Endorsements

Even though I have known Pastors Philip and Michelle Steele for several years now, I didn't know the woman she described in this powerful new book.

My first thought after reading it was that it is undoubtedly true that the love of God and the power of the Holy Spirit can transform a life when a person is willing to accept them.

Michelle is living proof of this, and I commend her for being so open and transparent as she told her story. I know her testimony of the life-change she experienced will minister to multitudes of others.

No matter how deep down into the pits of darkness people may find themselves, God's love is capable of reaching that far. Once again, Michelle's story proves this to be true.

I pray that as you read this book, if you identify with the hopelessness Michelle experienced, then do what she did. Look to God and ask His Son, Jesus, to come into your life as she did.

There is hope! There is a way out, and His name is Jesus!

Dr. Jerry Savelle
Crowley, Texas
Jerry Savelle Ministries International
www.JSMI.org

T0052044

I have known Michelle Steele for many years, and she is a true, dedicated woman of God. *Escaping Hell* is a "how-to" guide on staying free from a past of darkness and putting God first. How can someone escape a past of drug abuse and prostitution and become a pastor's wife and skilled Bible teacher and much more? Michelle's incredible book is a must-read! Once you pick it up, you won't be able to put it down.

DR. PAT HARRISON
Tulsa, Oklahoma
Co-Founder and President of Faith
Christian Fellowship International
www.fcf.org

Although I never knew the Michelle that is described in the first half of this book, my wife, Jeanne, and I have known the "new" Michelle for several years now. If you would like proof of how Jesus completely transforms a life, this book is a must-read!

PASTOR HAPPY CALDWELL
Little Rock, Arkansas
Founder and President of Victory Television Network
www.vtntv.com

ESCAPING
HELL

A TRUE STORY

GOD'S MIRACULOUS POWER
TO RESTORE A LIFE BENT
ON DESTRUCTION

MICHELLE STEELE

© Copyright 2022–Michelle Steele

Published by Harrison House Publishers
Shippensburg, PA 17257

ISBN 13 TP: 978-1-6803-1911-8
ISBN 13 eBook: 978-1-6803-1912-5
ISBN 13 HC: 978-1-6803-1914-9
ISBN 13 LP: 978-1-6803-1913-2

For Worldwide Distribution, Printed in the U.S.A.
2 3 4 5 6 7 8 / 26 25 24 23 22

DEDICATION

This book is dedicated to my husband. Philip, you have loved me unconditionally. When I couldn't see any value in myself, you loved me as if I was your priceless treasure. Your example of love, generosity, and forgiveness are a living expression of my Heavenly Father. Thank you for being a man who walks with God.

CONTENTS

FOREWORD

AMAZING TRANSFORMATION! These two words capture the essence of Michelle Steele's life.

This book is riveting, not only because it is a well-written story of the full extent that the hold of darkness had on a young woman's life, but because of the living proof of the transforming power of Jesus Christ and His Word.

Over the years I have met several Christians who came to Jesus out of desperate circumstances. I thank God for their deliverance! But they were still struggling years later, dealing with their past and the trauma it had inflicted. Why is Michelle Steele's life different from theirs? Is she special? Does God love her best? How does a drug addict and a prostitute become a pastor's wife, mother, a skilled Bible teacher, co-pastor of two churches, and an author of 10 books?

She put the Word of God first in her life by declaring it and acting upon it continually. By my observation, she still does.

In this book, she shares specific keys to overcoming the past and walking forward to freedom. The answer lies not in our feelings but in believing what God has said about us. We truly are who He says we are, and we can do what He says we can do. The past and *feelings* of failure are not the authority dominating our lives, the Word of God is the *final authority.* Michelle will show you how to get to the place of *believing, receiving, and attaining* victorious success in your life. It does not matter whether your background is tainted with sin or you are an avid churchgoer, the principles in this book apply to YOU!

When I first met Michelle, she had contacted our ministry offering to translate some of our books into the Spanish language. I wondered who this person might be and what her qualifications were, so I went on a search and found a website with a video of her teaching. (Correctly translating "what Charles Capps meant when he said that???" can be more than challenging when you aren't familiar with how a farmer from Arkansas *talks* and *what* his real message is!)

To my amazement, I found a powerful woman of God, teaching God's Word much like my father did; only without the southern farmer accent! As I listened, I was impressed with her knowledge of the scriptures and fascinated that she had taught herself to speak and preach in Spanish because that is what the Holy Spirit had instructed her to do.

Not only did Michelle translate our books, but she asked me to be a guest on her television show in Little Rock, Arkansas, where we found that we had a real "synergy" as we shared the life-changing power of the Word of God. We received so much positive response from these programs that we have continued producing and broadcasting new programs.

Philip and Michelle Steele invited me to speak at their churches in Kansas and Arkansas and a deep friendship developed. I found skilled and anointed pastors who shepherded their sheep into strong believers and also encouraged the flow of the Holy Spirit in their services. The health of their churches was additional confirmation that these pastors were teaching the Word to their people.

So you see, the Michelle I knew was so far removed from the Michelle of the past that I couldn't really reconcile the two in my mind. And really there is no reconciling the two. One of those people is dead. Dead to sin. Dead to what was and what has been. The other is truly alive unto God. She has committed herself to her Lord and Savior and His Word. She belongs to Him.

This is what it means to be a "new creature in Christ Jesus." The life lived in the flesh is dead, it was crucified on the cross. What was resurrected was the "new Michelle." A second chance? Yes. But not only a second chance, a new life.

Wherever your life has taken you, no matter how far away from God you have run, YOU ARE NOT TOO FAR GONE FOR GOD!

Michelle Steele is proof of that.

ANNETTE CAPPS
President, Capps Ministries
Broken Arrow, Oklahoma
February 20, 2022

CHAPTER ONE

THE FORCE OF
DESTRUCTION

Once upon a time, there was a man who found himself in a place he never intended to be. Night and day, the miserable existence that some called "life" inflicted such guilt, agony, and torment upon this man that he took sharp stones and rusty metal to carve deep gashes in his skin that matched the wounds in his soul.

He lived in a graveyard, wandering among the tombs, and stumbling in the darkness, he wailed mournful, animal-like shrieks. Hanging from his wrists and rubbing blisters around his ankles were the restraints of his family and friends who had tried to stop his self-destructive behavior.

No one could restrain him. The love of his family couldn't wash away the stain of his mistakes, and the condolences of his friends didn't ease the burden of his guilt. His life was set to self-destruct.

"But when he saw Jesus afar off...." The Bible tells us in Mark 5:6 that this filthy, demon-possessed man ran to

Jesus and began to worship Him. Years of guilt, shame, and destruction were cleansed in a moment, and this man found himself in his right mind.

This story illustrates the pain of the first twenty-three years of my life. As a young teenage girl, I made wrong decision after wrong decision. I made trouble at home, trouble at school, and trouble in my family.

The real trouble was the self-destructing pain on the inside of me. From the age of fifteen until I turned twenty-three, I ran through the tombs and hid in the mountains of drug addiction and criminal activity.

My family tried to pull me back to safety. I broke free from their love by lashing out at their compassion. I destroyed the relationships and the trust of the few people on this earth who really cared about me. My name is Michelle Steele, and this is my story.

My teeth were grinding together. My jaw was twitching as I sprinkled the precious white powder into the cap of the syringe. I pulled up just the right amount of water and added it to the powder in the cap. I pulled the liquid cocaine into the syringe and tapped the air to the top.

The sounds of the Sunday afternoon customers in the bar where I was secretly shooting dope were soon drowned out by the anticipated sound of the trains that came thundering through my head as my heart answered the call of the cocaine by pumping blood through my body at an outrageous pace.

Added to the strong dose of cocaine was the fact that I had been shooting dope nonstop since Friday night. Every time I took a shot, I asked the man supplying my drugs to put more cocaine in my spoon because I couldn't feel the rush the way I wanted to feel it. Days without food or sleep and a constant increase of cocaine proved to be a recipe for disaster.

Perhaps, that is why I slipped out of consciousness before I could even untie the belt from my left arm. It could be why my heart stopped beating, and my breath left my body.

Darkness surrounded me, a darkness that felt evil and oppressive. Suddenly, I was standing in front of a skull. But it was not an entire skeleton, just an enormous skull that stood as tall as me. I felt hands reaching from the darkness grasping for me, trying to pull me into the skull. They were hands of darkness, not black in color—it was the darkness stretching out its arms, reaching with its fingers to get a grip on me to draw me into death.

I experienced fear in a way I had never experienced fear before that moment. In that instant, I realized I wasn't ready to die. I didn't want the darkness to succeed in reaching me. In fear, I turned and ran. I ran back to my body.

The man performing CPR on my lifeless body was shocked. One minute he was desperately trying to get my heart to beat again. The next minute, he found himself fighting a frantic, panicked, half-crazed girl. I fought as if those hands were still reaching for me.

I ran from the back room of the bar and down the streets of the inner city in Nashville, Tennessee. When my friends from the bar caught up with me, I stood bewildered in the middle of the street. The cold rain gently fell as I shivered in fright, the blood still dripping from my arm.

I went to hell, and hell was real.

CHAPTER TWO

A DEAD-END STREET

I was in a graveyard of addiction, guilt, and destruction. You could have peered into the dark, eerie tombs of my drug addiction and seen a wasted, hopeless girl. Perhaps, you would've concluded that this prostitute would never move beyond the street to make anything out of her life. No one who knew me ever expected me to make it out alive.

How did I end up living on a dead-end street—in a place I never intended to be? I never dreamed of being a junkie, selling my body to supply the demands of the drug that was slowly killing me. I lived life in the fast lane of addiction and crime. Although my family tried to redirect me, I broke free from their love and destroyed the trust of the few people on this earth who really cared about me.

My mother and father both grew up and fell in love in a small, eastern Tennessee town called Greeneville. My father enlisted in the Army soon after they married and took my mother to Maryland, where my brother was born.

A couple of years later, they found themselves stationed in Frankfurt, Germany, where I made my grand appearance. My mother tells stories about how I was the most beautiful child in the Army hospital. She insists that everyone could recognize that there was something special about me. Isn't that what every mother says?

I was still very young when my parents moved back to Tennessee. My father had completed his time in the Army, and we moved around a few times until we settled in Nashville. Dad worked with computers, and my mom stayed home with my brother and me.

Life looked good through my little kindergarten eyes. I played in the sandbox behind our home and chased lightning bugs in the dusk. Every Friday night was pizza night, and Saturday mornings were spent watching Bugs Bunny and Wiley Coyote cartoons.

I loved my parents and thought things were perfect until I woke up one night to hear my mother sobbing and my father's drunken ranting. I stood in the doorway of my room and trembled in the twilight as my perfect world came undone.

By the time I was in first grade, my parents had divorced. My brother and I were sent to live with my grandparents in East Tennessee. We saw our parents when they came to visit for holidays. Neither of us understood why our entire lives had completely changed.

We lived on the farm with my grandparents for a few years until my dad remarried. Dad brought us to live with him, his new wife, and her daughter, who was slightly younger than me. My brother and I had weekly visits with our mom, who had remarried and lived about forty-five minutes from our new home.

I attended great schools and lived in an affluent suburb, surrounded by country music singers and Grand Ole Opry stars. I was a rich kid, raised in the lap of luxury. I learned to drive in my stepmother's Mercedes, had a pool in my backyard, and lived in a gorgeous home. Yet, I turned down a path that led to destruction.

A Pattern of Undeserved Guilt

It seemed like a normal, average life except for the self-destructive force overshadowing my life. What should have been happy kept turning out sad, and what should have been right kept turning out wrong.

In sixth grade, I attended a church with a girl from school who invited me. I went there for about a year, sang in the youth choir, and even went on a trip with the choir to Panama City Beach.

There was an eighteen-year-old guy there who drove a shiny, black Trans Am. He had a girlfriend, but he talked to me when she wasn't around. He was one of the few people who acknowledged I was there.

He called me a few times and wanted to meet me. How was I supposed to know that he was only talking to me to get alone with me? I was thirteen years old when he coerced me to have sex. I didn't know anything about sex. I was a sixth-grader! I didn't desire it, and I wasn't "turned on." I was pressured to do it. After he had sex with me, he wouldn't talk to me anymore. When his girlfriend found out, they both acted like I was the guilty one who made him do something. I didn't go back to church again for many years.

Pressure to Perform

When I was about thirteen, my parents bought a Tennessee Walking horse for my stepsister and me to ride. I was thrilled! The barn was within walking distance of our home, and I would spend hours there around the horses.

There was an older man who worked around the barn. He owned a horse there—a mustang that could run like the wind, and he offered to let me ride it whenever I wanted. But I was too naïve to realize that this man was using the mustang to get me into a compromising position.

One day, he invited me to go with him to look at some other wild mustangs he was interested in buying. He made it seem so innocent and fun. My parents let me go on this expedition, knowing how excited I was about horses. It wasn't until we were over an hour into our trip that I realized something wasn't quite right.

The man was blurry-eyed and slurring his speech. He reached over the cab of the pickup truck and started rubbing my leg, reaching in between my legs. I was terrified. All

I knew to do was scoot as far as possible toward the passenger-side door and silently shiver in fear.

This made him angry, and his anger was torment. He remained angry with me for the rest of the trip. For a young girl who thrived on pleasing people, needing their approval, this anger became a heavy burden of guilt that followed me throughout my young life. *What did I do? Why is he mad at me?* My parents never knew what had happened. Somehow, I was afraid that if I told them, *I* would be in trouble. Soon, I started avoiding the barn for fear of running into him. Since I wasn't taking care of the horse, feeding, or riding her regularly, my parents ended up selling her.

The next year, I started junior high school. The seventh and eighth-grade football coach taught health classes. In class, he would let the cheerleaders and the most beautiful girls sit at his desk to help him grade papers. To a young freshman who wanted to fit in, it seemed like a place of status—a position of importance.

In the second semester, I was one of the "chosen" who sat at the desk to grade papers. Somehow in conversation, the coach found out that I loved horses and invited me to join him and some friends to ride horses in the snow. When the day came, I was the only one there to ride. I thought, *Here we go again. Now, what do I do?*

I didn't want to make the coach mad at me. So, when he began touching me, I cringed and screamed silently but didn't move. When he put his big, mustached lips on me and kissed me, I was horrified and tried desperately to think of a way to escape, but I couldn't find a way out without making him angry.

Again, I *thought* I couldn't tell anybody because I was afraid that *I* would get in trouble. I felt guilty, like I had done something wrong, and I was tormented.

Finally, I got up the nerve to go to the principal and share what had happened. As I sat in the outer office waiting for a meeting with him, I was stunned when the coach and the principal exited the office on their way to an afternoon golf game.

I knew my words would be in vain. As he saw me seated there, the coach delivered a steely, cold warning with his eyes. From that moment, something happened in my heart. I accepted the guilt of his sin and began to hate myself. A pattern of self-destruction began.

Self-Medication and Self-Mutilation

The inner turmoil of my shame and guilt began to poison every area of my life. I turned to music to medicate my pain and found solace in heavy metal lyrics that promised suicide was the solution. I immersed myself in the rebellion and anguish I encountered in those songs.

Within months, I found myself searching the utility drawer in the house for a razor blade and locked myself in the bathroom, trying to slice my wrist. I managed to draw blood but didn't go deep enough to kill myself. No one ever knew that I had tried. While I still have the scars on my wrist, no one ever noticed the wounds on my fourteen-year-old arm.

I hid in the closet and prayed to Satan to use my life. I prayed for the devil to make me glamorous and sexy like the images I saw in my dad's porn magazines. I didn't even know how to pray to God, but I figured out how to pray to the devil through the songs I listened to and the books they led me to read.

My parents began taking me to see a psychiatrist. I hated every session. Of course, he wanted to talk about the home life and my past and what could have happened to bring me to this place of destruction. I blamed my parents for getting a divorce, and I blamed my stepmother for everything going wrong in my life. I told the psychiatrist everything but the truth. By now, I was convinced that something about me was bent toward the wrong side of the tracks.

I ended up in the psych ward of the hospital when I was in ninth grade and began taking anti-depression medications. When I was released, I overdosed on them and nearly died. But nobody knew. They just thought I was sick and needed to sleep.

I began looking for acceptance with the tough kids at school. Since we had never lived anywhere long enough for me to develop friendships, I had no idea how to fit in with anyone. I just tried to be tougher and crazier than the rest. I learned to drink the most, cuss the loudest, and take the biggest risks.

My parents would drop me off at the mall, and I would meet up with some older boys who took us out to get high and party. I lied to my parents about where I was going and went to rock concerts. I honestly don't remember any of the concerts because I was drunk or stoned by the time the music started.

During this time, I met a lot of older boys who took advantage of my youthful rebellion. It was easy for guys to get me to sleep with them because I didn't want to make them mad by saying no. Many times, a guy would make me feel like I had to go all of the way. If I started making out with him, he would pressure me to "finish what I started."

Little by little, I was being programmed to give away what I didn't want to give for someone else's pleasure. These guys made it plain that they expected something in return for the money they spent on a movie and dinner. But, most of the time, I was never treated that well. I would just sneak out of my room at night and have people pick me up down the road. I became that girl that was crazy enough to try anything.

A Teenage Runaway

I was crazy enough to run away from home as soon as I turned sixteen and got a car. I intended to go to California and get a job. I made it as far as Phoenix, Arizona, before the boy who ran with me took *my* money and bought himself a bus ticket back home.

A nice lady who found me crying on the sidewalk outside of a hotel gave me enough money to drive to Fort Smith,

Arkansas, where a friend I knew from junior high school had moved. But in Arkansas, my parents tracked me down and took the car. I hid in the attic of her house until nightfall. She bought a bus ticket to send me to Detroit, where I knew a friend.

Detroit was a crazy, dangerous place for a sixteen-year-old runaway. It was in Detroit that I broke down and called my granddaddy in the middle of the night. He said, "Girl, what are you doing? Get yourself back home!" I caught a bus back to Nashville.

But my return home was short-lived because the next morning, I was placed in a mental hospital for adolescents. I was so mad that I had come back just to be locked up. I wasn't the only one who didn't want to be locked up in that facility.

I heard a guy making plans. Earlier that morning, a patient had become angry and slammed her fist into the window. The window shattered because it was plain glass instead of reinforced glass. This guy was talking about breaking another window and escaping that night.

The girl who was my roommate didn't want to leave, but she was willing to be the diversion so that we could make a clean break. Late that night, the two guys crawled into our room. My roommate went to the nurse's desk, saying she felt sick. We pushed a bed in front of the door, and I poured a whole bottle of liquid hairspray on the bed and lit a match.

The guys picked up a nightstand and threw it against the window. But this window didn't shatter as we expected.

It was reinforced glass. After a few more times of bashing the window with the nightstand, the glass had fragmented enough that we were finally able to push it out of the frame and jump out onto the ground. We were on the run!

We went to an area in East Nashville where I knew some students of a diesel college. Party animals! I stayed there with them for a few weeks. The house was a typical, college party house with people smoking pot and getting drunk all the time.

One of the men that lived there had a girlfriend who was nearer to my age. I told her about my parents' house and how rich my parents were. We decided to walk there and hide in the shed all night behind my parent's house and wait until they left for work the next day. We broke into the house and took jewelry from my stepmother's jewelry box.

After walking all of the way back to Nashville, this girl claimed to know someone who could sell it. Her friends took us to a convenience store on the other side of town and told us to wait there while they went down the street to sell it. They never came back. (Did I mention how naïve I really was?)

I found out how to sell my plasma while I was there. I sold my plasma to buy a concert ticket to a rock group. Before the concert, I drank peppermint Schnapps for the first time. I got so wasted! I barely remember the concert. I lost the people that I had gone with, and I am not sure how I got back to where I was staying.

A Second Chance

A few days later, I walked up to the business that my mom and stepdad owned to say "hello." This whole time I had been hiding just a few blocks from their shoe repair shop. My mom was glad to see me, and Jim offered to buy me a sandwich from the deli next door. I was so naïve that I missed their silent signals to each other.

While he was next door, he called the police and reported me. My heart sank as I watched the police pull up in front of their store. I felt betrayed as I looked at my mom and realized that my first contact with her in months was going to end with me in handcuffs. I left there in the back of the police car.

I spent the night in the Sumner County Adult Detention Center, awaiting an appearance before a judge. When I appeared before the judge, I requested that custody be removed from my dad and stepmother. Instead, the judge placed me in a group home with about eight other girls, and I settled into my new life.

I went to high school and lived in the group home for a long while. My grades were good, and I thrived in the structured environment. I joined the choral group of the high school and made new friends. I really enjoyed eleventh grade. I went to the junior prom and even traveled to New York City with the choral group to see *Cats* on Broadway. I had some weekend visits with my parents, and we were working toward restoration.

But it was during my time in the group home that I started getting letters from a guy named "Bo." I had met him a year earlier through a friend in my junior high school. Since I was known around school as a wild girl, my friend thought Bo and I would have some things in common. He was so "wild" that while he was dating her, he was asking her to set him up with other girls. The crazy thing is that she was actually doing it.

I had talked to Bo on the phone a few times. At first I thought, *What an arrogant guy!* He wanted to talk about sex and about how tough he was. But it was the challenge in his voice that pushed me to meet him. He dared me to prove myself by playing the "suburbanite girl is too good to come to East Nashville" game. He used tactics like, "You're too scared. You're just a tease. You're just like a Sumner County girl, all talk and no action." He was bold, dangerous, and very sure of himself.

Bo was known around his part of town to be the tough guy. All of the girls wanted him, and he knew it. He had the rock star, bad-guy look with long, jet-black hair and steel blue eyes. He walked into a room, strutting around like he was looking for trouble. The guys around town were afraid of him, and the girls were intrigued with him.

I still don't know how he discovered I was in the group home or how he got the address to write to me. Bo was locked up in a maximum-security facility for juveniles serving a sentence for strong-armed robbery. In his letters, he talked as if we were girlfriend and boyfriend. He wrote things like, "I can't stand the thought of *my girl* being locked up." His letters came on a regular basis, and I was won over by the attention. I had never had anyone show that kind of interest in me, wanting to be my boyfriend. We stayed in touch and ended up being released about the same time.

The group home released me back to my parents. It seemed so difficult to be at home after all the lies I had told and the distrust I had caused. But my stepmother gave me a job in her company, and they bought another car for me to drive. We tried to return to normal. But the force of destruction was still raging in my life.

I wasn't addicted to drugs or alcohol. I was just convinced that I didn't deserve anything good and determined to punish myself by pushing away those who I should have reached for. I was reaching for the ones who didn't care about me but wanted to use me.

I began talking to Bo on the phone and went to visit him at his grandmother's house a few times. The first time I went over, Bo was next door at his dad's house. It wasn't your normal family situation where a responsible dad is around. Bo's dad encouraged Bo's illegal behavior.

Bo's father sent me around to the side of the house after looking me over with a hungry look. His dad had an old bus that was turned into a camper. It was like a party house on wheels. Bo had paint around his mouth and was acting strange.

I didn't know what "huffing" was all about, but I soon figured it out. Bo kissed me, and his mouth tasted like spray paint. He encouraged me to try, and I did it once or twice. After the initial hallucination, my stomach felt like I had ridden too many roller coasters, and my head hurt. I didn't stay long.

He called me to come out again. I met up with Bo and ended up driving him around East Nashville to find pot and drink beer. I had stolen money from my stepmother and stayed out without any word where I was.

When they confronted me, I threatened to run away again. I wasn't really serious, but my mouth kept talking, and my pride kept rebelling. My parents let me leave. "Just don't take the car," was their response.

Bo was shocked when I showed up on his doorstep the next day. Actually, it was his grandma's doorstep. I told him I had nowhere to go. We were both only sixteen years old.

Chapter Three

Burning Bridges

A nne Cosby let me move in with the understanding that I would sleep in a separate area and go to work to pay some rent. I went to work as a waitress at a restaurant down the street.

I worked with a girl named Tina, who knew Bo from school. Instead of waiting for me to get off work, Bo would leave with her when she got off earlier than I did.

We argued about the fact that he was spending so much time with Tina, and I soon discovered that he was not interested in being a one-woman man. We argued, and the argument escalated into a fight. Bo slapped me a few times before throwing all my belongings into the back of Anne's old truck. He left, and I was stranded, trying to decide what to do.

Well, when Anne came home, she saw all my belongings thrown in her truck and asked, "Why does *he* think he can throw you out of *my* house?" She helped me move my meager possessions back into the room I was renting.

Right then, I should have realized that I shouldn't stay with a man who would hit me. But I didn't have a clue about domestic violence. I didn't know anything about abuse. I had no one to turn to and nowhere to go. I didn't feel like I could go home or turn to my mother. Their answer to my problem was to lock me up or give me antidepressants.

When he came back around wanting to sleep with me or get money from me, I was glad to have him back. But my decision to go back to him was like saying, "You put your hands on me, and I allowed it. Now I'm staying for more."

I waited tables until closing every night and tried to attend school during the day. But it was a totally different experience at this school. I went from being an A and B student in a suburban school to failing my classes in an inner-city school. I felt out of place. Add to that the fact that I worked late into the night, and I kept falling asleep in class. I dropped out of my senior year of high school.

Bo was going back to the juvenile detention center for about a year for the armed robbery he had committed. At first, he was incarcerated in a medium-security facility near Pikeville, Tennessee, which was far from Nashville. We could only go see him about once a month or so.

But one Saturday morning, Anne took me out and said she had a surprise for me. We drove up the highway toward an area on the outskirts of Nashville called Ashland City. As we pulled off the exit, she explained that Bo had been transferred to a minimum-security facility here close to us. We visited with Bo and found out that he could earn weekend passes for good behavior.

On the first weekend that Bo earned a weekend pass, he took some of the money I had earned to buy a $100 car. He spent all his weekend working on that pitiful car until he got it running. I didn't know the plan he was formulating in his mind.

Jail Break

The next week, he called me and told me to drive up the street by the detention center very slowly. I realized what he was asking me to do, and it scared me senseless. He instructed me to pack our clothes and bring all my money. I did as he instructed and drove up the street slowly, listening and looking. Nothing happened, so I drove back to Anne's house, trying to act like nothing was out of the ordinary.

Bo called as soon as I entered the house. He said, "Come back up by the detention center. Drive slowly by the side of the road with your lights off. Listen for me to whistle."

I traveled back up the highway and turned onto the road that led to the detention center. My palms were sweating, and my stomach was churning as I turned the headlights off and drove slowly down the street in the dark with my windows rolled down.

Sure enough, a low, soft whistle cut through the silent country evening, and out of the darkness, Bo and another kid came rushing toward the car. They jumped in and slid down in the seats while Bo encouraged me to drive as normally as possible.

Now what? We are officially on the run with just a little bit of money. Bo talked me into calling my dad and asking him for money to come to Florida. While I hadn't really stayed in touch with Dad, I found out that he and Sharon had divorced and that he had moved to Orlando.

When I called my dad, he was surprised. He agreed to give me money and let us stay with him for a few weeks. He didn't even ask me why the big hurry. He called a friend of his in Nashville who met us with some cash and filled up our tank. We headed out across the country in a junk car we had purchased for $100. We were on the run from the police!

We arrived in Florida with big plans to get jobs and get an apartment. At least, I thought those were our plans. Above the gas money, my dad gave us around five hundred more dollars to get an apartment, so we started looking for jobs and checking out apartments. Bo couldn't give his social security number or real name because he was on the run, so we were having a hard time finding jobs.

At this time, I didn't drink much or do any excessive drugs. I smoked some pot here or there and was satisfied enough with that. But Bo had a different appetite.

One day, when he was supposed to be looking for a job, Bo managed to purchase some morphine and syringes. He brought them back to my dad's apartment along with a huge bag of "serious" reefer, and we sat around getting high instead of looking for a job.

My dad confronted us one afternoon, but we were too stoned to even respond to his conversation. He told us to keep the money and find somewhere else to stay.

We packed our bags and left that night, not exactly sure where we would go. Bo had been locked up with someone who lived up in Michigan, so we headed in that direction. We were driving from Orlando, Florida, to Michigan in a $100 car that wasn't fit for the road!

We came through Nashville on our way and stayed at a friend's apartment. We used some of the money that we had left over from what my dad had given us to get some drugs from the projects.

This was my second experience with a needle. We found what was called "tees and blues." These two pills were used for heart patients, but we mixed them together and injected them.

These pills were so chalky that we had to tear up a cigarette filter to use to draw the drugs through to avoid getting all of the chalk in our syringes. We got high that night with Bo's friends and left in the morning.

We still had the young guy that broke out with Bo traveling with us. He wasn't any trouble except when Bo wanted to have sex, and then, three was a crowd. The three of us stopped in Kentucky that night and spent some of our money on a hotel room.

I was so tired that I could barely keep my eyes open! Bo had other things on his mind, but I was so wiped out that I ruined his plans. He became angry and mean about what he expected of me. I thought, *Here we go with guilt and expectations again.* I began to form an understanding that my value as a woman was based on the level of performance to a man's expectations.

In other words, I was only worth something if I gave him what he wanted. But the problem was that "what he wanted" kept changing. I could never keep up with the demands.

We drove up to Michigan only to find out that the young man who Bo knew had gone out of town to stay with his mother. The guy's father let us spend the night on the floor and made us breakfast in the morning. We had arrived in the midst of a snowstorm and had no clothing for the cold. The man felt sorry for us and gave us blankets and some old jackets as we set for who knows where.

We drove until we ran out of money and fuel. We left the title in that $100 car for whoever found it and set out walking in the cold snowstorm.

I was sick and exhausted. I looked pitiful, but I felt even worse than I looked. I stood freezing on the side of a cold, wet highway, wondering, *What have I got myself into?*

Is this what I ran away from home to experience? I escaped the rules and government of my parents and school only to be miserable and cold in the middle of nowhere.

Bo called his family from the warmth of a truck stop. I remember hearing him complaining to his mom that I was no fun. He said, "She is sick all the time and only wants to sleep."

His mother opened his eyes and mine to the facts of life. "Son, she is probably pregnant!" Bo's father agreed to buy us some bus tickets home, and Bo's friend called his parents and headed home too.

Alone on the Mountain

Since we were still on the run, Bo's family prepared us a place to live on some property in the country that Bo's dad owned. It was an old trailer with no electricity or water on the top of this mountain in Ashland City. They fixed a wood-burning stove for us to use to cook and stay warm and hung blankets as walls to keep the heat in one area.

Bo's grandmother sent us some of the chickens out of her freezer that she had killed and plucked herself. She sent a box filled with welfare rice and tuna along with condiments and ramen noodles.

Remember, I was raised in the suburbs. I had done some cooking in our kitchen, and I could follow a recipe. But I didn't know how to start a fire, and I didn't know how to cut up a chicken. I didn't know how to make coffee without a coffee maker. Well, Bo didn't know much either. Let's just say, welfare tuna and rice make the nastiest combination ever!

We stayed in that cold, dreary hideaway until winter broke. Bo went to work in construction so that he could get paid without reporting taxes. With his first paycheck, Bo bought a motorcycle to ride back and forth to work.

While Bo went to work every day, I was stuck on that mountain, experiencing all of the changes that a pregnant woman goes through. But I didn't have anyone around to explain what was happening as my body changed. I didn't have any television or telephone to keep me connected with the world. We did manage to get some electricity turned on and had a stereo, lights, and a hot plate for cooking.

Bo wasn't ready for a family or any responsibility. Just like most sixteen-year-olds, he was ready to party. Even though we were "on the run," he became braver and braver about being in public and less interested in hiding out in a nasty trailer with a young pregnant girl who had no access to a shower or makeup.

One day, about three weeks after he had started working, Bo said, "I'm going to go get some hamburgers." I had only been off the mountain once or twice since we came back to the Nashville area. I was ready to get out of there. Immediately I jumped up, ready to go. Bo told me, "No, you stay here, and I'll be right back."

My heart wanted to keep the hope that he cared for me and would return. I kept myself busy for a few days waiting for him to return with his excuse or reasons why it had taken him so long to return. I would have believed anything.

I waited an entire week before I walked off that mountain to search for him. I was out of food and drinking water and hadn't spoken to anyone in too long.

After walking an entire day, I reached civilization. I went to his sister's house because it was the closest. I was worried that Bo had been caught and put back in jail.

Instead, I found him eating a peanut butter sandwich and sitting on his sister's couch. I was speechless and stupid. I asked him, "Where have you been? Why haven't you come back for me?"

He never moved from the couch. He looked at me with disinterest and replied, "Don't you get it? I don't want you around."

I felt like I had been punched in the chest. I had risked my freedom to break him out of the detention center. I lost my job to run across the country. I had ruined my relationship with my dad by borrowing money and getting high with it. I had suffered alone for weeks in a freezing, miserable trailer because he was on the run, and now this. I left there and headed to his grandmother's house. All my belongings were still there since the day that I had broken Bo out of prison.

Bo's grandmother, Anne, was quite a character. She was known for her independence and, sometimes, her stubbornness. Above all, Anne was an advocate for the down and out. When Anne heard everything that had occurred, she moved me back into her home. "Just let him go on, then. You don't need him."

With the advice of Bo's sister, I went to the free county clinic and signed up for prenatal care. I had to sign up for welfare to get health care for the birth of the baby. I had never heard of WIC and had no earthly idea how the welfare system worked. They signed me up for everything. I had everything in place to receive a check, welfare cheese, and food stamps, too.

My Ex-Best Friend

I went to work as a waitress at Pizza Hut and as a cashier at a juice stand in the mall. I worked my two jobs and saved my money.

The next time I saw Bo was when he came by to see his dad, who lived next door. When I saw the car that he was driving and the girl he was with, I was infuriated! The girl who was now his girlfriend had been my best friend in junior high school. I am pregnant with his baby, and he's sleeping with my ex-best friend!

Little by little, Bo began making his way back into my life. He would drop by the place I worked in the mall to order a smoothie to mix his vodka in. He would come by his grandmother's house and talk to me.

Before long, he was doing more than just talking. He began to figure out that he could "have his cake and eat it too." Bo reassured me that this girl didn't mean that much to him. As a matter of fact, he had convinced her to work at a "massage parlor" in town.

So, while she was turning tricks in this massage parlor, he was out at the bars, drinking and having a great time. He continually came around while she was "working," and he had sex with me. I was so desperate to have him back that I convinced myself this was just the first step to drawing him back.

I was thinking about moving back to Hendersonville. So, I searched and found an apartment that I could afford with the money I had saved and moved. Because Bo still had the ability to wrap me around his little finger, I ended up allowing him and his girlfriend to move into my new apartment. Go ahead and say it—"How stupid!"

But Bo had plans for me. When his girlfriend was around, he acted one way. When she was gone, he acted like we were still an item. He began to drop subtle hints about how I could be with him again.

He started by telling me how stupid it was for me to be working two jobs while I was pregnant. He said that I could make more money with less effort if I went to work with him. He had a new scheme in mind, and little by little, Bo explained his plans to me.

CHAPTER FOUR

SOUTHERN COMFORT

It seemed like a script from a soap opera, only worse! *How could I really be going through with this?* This was the thought racing through my mind as I stepped out of the car and made my way across the parking lot.

It was a dead giveaway for a female to leave a vehicle parked in the "auto" section to go strolling down through the long line of eighteen-wheelers in the parking lot of the truck stop. Of course, the fact that I was dressed in tight, black spandex that accentuated every curve of my sixteen-year-old body didn't help matters.

This was my first experience as a prostitute, so I rehearsed the detailed instructions I had been given as I walked. I went over the details of what I was supposed to say when a trucker rolled down his window and how to negotiate the price as I sat in the cab of the truck. In all his instructions, Bo neglected to explain how I was supposed to live with myself after selling my body.

With every step, I braced myself, attempting to suffocate the fear of what I was about to do. I was afraid of everything about this situation. I was afraid of being arrested by the police, afraid of having sex with strange men, and afraid of losing Bo forever.

Little by little, Bo had unfolded his plan to me. While seducing me with the promise of being "his girl" again, he revealed what he needed me to do. He wanted me to "work" at the truck stop with his girlfriend.

He assured me that she meant nothing to him, but he wanted me to play along so that he could keep her working. I convinced myself that if I played this game, I could make him love me again. I wanted the romance of that guy who wrote me letters, wanting to protect me when I was in the group home.

The thought that should have been crystal clear, I continually shoved to the back of my mind. *How could you ever trust the love of a guy that would make you sell your body while you are pregnant with his child?*

Please realize that Bo never forced me to do anything. I could have stayed on my normal job, lived with his grandmother, and gone on with my life. As an adult, I realize the choices that I could have made.

But in the moment, I didn't see any other options, and there were no other influences in my life urging me to look at my responsibilities. Only one person "had my ear."

If you are reading this and you feel trapped, hear me as I plead with you: Think about your future and don't throw your life away! Please find a responsible person who can speak some words of wisdom to you. Don't make permanent decisions in a temporary situation! Reach outside of the circle of people who are pressuring you and ask God to help you see the bigger picture.

The first truck that I climbed into marked the beginning of a long, shame-filled road of prostitution. In the smoky, dimly lit cab of a truck, I began selling my services over the airwaves.

My first "handle" on the CB radio became "Southern Comfort." With my young, sweet, little southern drawl, I would interrupt the trucker's talk to introduce myself. "Breaker, breaker 1-9. This is Southern Comfort calling out to see who is interested in some company tonight. Kick it on back to Southern Comfort on channel 13." Then, I would turn the dial over to channel 13 and chat with the truckers who were interested, finding out their location and the description of their truck.

Pregnant and Prostituting

The saddest part of the whole situation was that as a sixteen-year-old pregnant girl, I made more money than the other girls on the lot. Bo's girlfriend didn't like the fact that Bo only took half of my money and took all of hers. Maybe there was an advantage to being "the other woman" after all.

The first time I was arrested for prostitution was at the truck stop. I had been warned that a local police officer patrolled the lot, and I should be on the lookout for any car lights when walking in the truck section.

The first few times that I saw him, I was in the safety of a truck. The truck drivers would hide me in their bunks as long as necessary. I even had some warn me that the cop was driving through, and I would climb under the trucks or hide behind them.

Eventually, my luck ran out, and I turned a corner and walked right into him. I received a citation and paid a $65 fine. The other working girls would joke that this was how we paid our taxes.

I stayed away from drugs the entire time that I was pregnant. When Bo and his girlfriend started shooting cocaine in the apartment, I became uncomfortable. Cocaine makes people act really paranoid, and their behavior becomes erratic.

I had never seen anyone mainline cocaine, and I was more than a little unnerved. At one point, he even tried to get me to join them. I became angry and refused. I wanted my baby to be born healthy. I am so thankful that I stood my ground. My firstborn daughter is truly worth it.

The whole situation was built for disaster. I didn't really speak to Bo's girlfriend. Bo had crazy ideas about trying to get us to have a threesome, but it wasn't happening.

I had the only bedroom since it was my apartment, so usually, they slept in the living room. One night, he marched her right in, and they climbed into my bed. I wasn't impressed when he tried to pull my hand over in the darkness to join them. I stayed on my side and minded my own business.

Three was a crowd, and soon, his drug partner won out. I was getting too big to keep working anyway. They went their own way and kept busy at the truck stop at night. Eventually, they traveled to Florida with a guy who promised them a connection to some great heroin.

I moved back in with Anne and began making preparations for the birth of my baby. Bo's family suggested that I call my mom and include her in the birth of my baby. I made the phone call and worked on repairing the relationship. She was able to be with me in the delivery when I gave birth.

My beautiful baby girl was born with features so perfect, like a living, fragile porcelain doll. I took her home to Anne's house and began to learn about midnight feedings and the other fun adventures experienced with a new baby.

Bo's mother was the first to hear from him, and she began telling him about his daughter and how beautiful she was. She encouraged Bo to come back to Nashville and put his name on the birth certificate as the legal father. Bo headed back from Florida. On the way back, he told his girlfriend, "I don't want you anymore." When he arrived back in Nashville, he acted as if we had never been apart.

"High-Class" Prostitution?

Would you laugh at me if I told you that I had hoped things would be different? Somewhere in my imaginary world, I thought having his baby would make me more valuable. Now, maybe he would want to settle down and be a family.

About six weeks after our baby was born, Bo told me about his new plan. I tried to talk him out of it, offering to go back to my job as a waitress.

I wanted to be home with my baby. I wanted to have a real life. But Bo had it all planned out. He said that we could get Anne or my mom to watch the baby. He wanted me to work for an escort service, moving my prostitution from the truck stops to the hotels.

The interview process for my first escort service was the weirdest experience in my life. The owner of the escort service required a "date" in order to check out the services you could offer. I had to lie and say that I was single with no boyfriend because Bo didn't want me to be disqualified from getting the job. I made it through the interview process.

Within the week, I was equipped with a beeper, a credit card machine, and my first "high-class" prostitution job. I drove myself in our junky car to exclusive hotels, climbed out in a sexy dress with a briefcase full of condoms. I pretended that no one knew what I was doing as I climbed into the elevator.

While I was working at night and sleeping all day, Bo enjoyed the benefits of my labor. He was free to drink, play guitar, and shoot pool with his friends. He enjoyed the nightlife with all of the perks, including sleeping around with whoever made themselves available to him.

I knew that Bo was with other women, and I was powerless to stop it. If I had a night off from work and went with him to the bar, I was treated as if I was "unwanted" company.

While drinking one night, we started a game of truth and dare with another couple. We were out in the country in an abandoned trailer with a fifth of whiskey and too much time on our hands. The other girl challenged me to "truth" as she began to tell me how often she had been with Bo in the last few weeks.

Bo became very uncomfortable because he expected me to turn on him. But, even in my drunken state, I still knew that I couldn't whip him. I turned on this girl instead.

Bo and his friend were quite amused by the fight and kept handing me things to use as I beat her. I held her down on the ground and beat her face against the carpet. All of the rage, shame, and frustration of my situation was taken out on her. With every punch of my fists, I was beating all of the other girls that had been with Bo. I was beating Bo for using me and degrading me.

We drove this girl back to town with her face bloody and swollen. The next day, her family came to the trailer park where we were staying with Bo's mom and said that this girl needed surgery to repair her eyes. To Bo, I was the hero. He bragged about me to his friends and family, recalling every blow and reliving every punch. But I wasn't celebrating. I was miserable.

Caught in the Middle

In the beginning, my mom and stepdad were the ones watching our daughter, and they became very attached to her. She lived with them constantly. They bought her everything she needed and outfitted their house and business with all of the things a new baby needed, including a walker, highchair, bed, dresser, clothes, etc.

They never complained about having her. If I came to get her and spend time with her, my mom was ready for her to come back as soon as I left the driveway.

But Bo's family began to grow concerned and started warning him that my mom might try to take custody of the baby. He became suspicious. It didn't help that ever since Bo heard about my mom and stepdad turning me in to the police when I was a runaway, he had never trusted them.

I was caught in the middle. I had brought her to them and asked for their help. Now, I was being pressured to take her away from them.

The decision was made for me after one drunken, crazy night. Bo was blind-running drunk, and I was well on my way.

If Bo was happy before he started drinking, then he could be a happy drunk. But, if he was angry or upset when he started drinking, he became belligerent and dangerous.

This was one of those nights, and I couldn't do anything right. Everything I said was wrong and stupid. As we left one of the sleazy bars on Dickerson Road, he was going to leave me.

He jumped into the car, and I jumped on the windshield. As quick as lightning, he was out of the car. He punched me in the head and threw me down in front of the car. I rolled out of the way at the last minute before he could drive over me.

I was unaware that he drove to my mom's house demanding that they give him the baby. It was two o'clock in the morning. My stepdad tried to reason with Bo, saying, "You've been drinking. The baby is asleep. You don't even have a car seat. Please come back tomorrow, Bo."

Thankfully, my stepdad stood his ground and didn't let Bo take her. Bo became violent and punched him in the nose. The blow struck my stepdad so hard that he fell back into the house. Bo was afraid that the police might be called and left immediately.

I called my mom's house from a payphone and asked her to send my stepdad to pick me up. I told her that I was hiding from Bo under some vehicles parked in front of a business. She told him where to pull up and wait for me.

When he came, I was so scared that Bo was watching from somewhere that I sunk down in the seat to hide. The next day, my mom and stepdad went to work, taking the baby to the shop with them. They told me I could stay as long as I needed. I think it lasted a day or two.

I had nothing. Everything I owned was at Anne's house. I called Anne to talk about getting my things, and she started telling me to bring the baby and come back. She convinced me that Bo was sorry and that we needed to work things out. I went back, and the baby was allowed to visit my mom less and less.

Although my relationship with Bo was rocky, he began to lean on me and depend on me. In his own way, I think he loved me.

When our daughter was a little over a year old, he asked me to marry him. He proposed to me on one knee, in the middle of the dance floor of a sleazy nightclub. He took the money that I had made prostituting the night before and bought a set of wedding rings from a pawn shop.

It was the moment I had been waiting for, and yet it lacked the victory and joy that I expected it to bring. He wanted to marry me, but he still wanted me to sell my body for a living. He wanted to marry me, but I wasn't valuable enough for me to be his and his only.

There was no beautiful wedding dress. There were no bridesmaids, no maid of honor, or best man. We got married in a courtroom, ate dinner in a cafeteria, and went to a park to smoke some skunkweed. I was so stoned that I drove the car into a ditch. What a memorable occasion!

CHAPTER FIVE

THE FIRST TIME I DIED

As I strolled down the side of the road, intending to look nonchalant and innocent, I scanned the cars for any sign of the police. I twisted my hips and flipped my hair as I looked for any sign of interest from the passing cars.

Nervously, I took a long hard drag on what was left of my cigarette before I flicked the still-smoking stub to the street. *I hate this!* I thought to myself. My stomach was twisted in knots because of my nerves. But I endured the anxiety for the hope of the high that awaited me. Bo promised that we would go straight to the projects to get our drugs as soon as I made thirty more dollars.

I wasn't used to being on Dickerson Road. Only the girls that couldn't make it anywhere else ended up here. This is where you end up when you have reached the bottom of the barrel. This is where the girls end up when they don't care anymore.

I realized that I had crossed that line. I didn't care anymore. I didn't care who saw me here. Well, I did. I cried about the thought of my kids in the car with Anne seeing me as they drove by. Even though they wouldn't know what I was doing right now, someday they would be old enough to know why Momma used to walk on Dickerson Road.

I cried when I thought of my mom or stepdad seeing me as they drove down the street to run an errand. I knew that my family was aware of what I did. It was just that no one ever came out and said anything. No one had ever looked me in the eyes and asked, "Michelle, are you out of your mind?"

From the age of sixteen, when I ran away from home, until this point in my life, as I walked through the most degrading place that a young girl can find herself, no one had broken through the self-disgust and convinced me that I was worth saving. From the time that I began climbing into the eighteen-wheeler, semi-trucks to sell my sixteen-year-old body for forty dollars, my belief system was strengthened in one thing: I believed that I was of little or no value.

Even when I learned how to "dress up all in lace and go in style," the high heels and sexy lingerie didn't help the brokenness in my soul. I walked through the lobbies of the finest hotels in Nashville, Tennessee. I rode up on elevators standing next to the prestigious and elite, only to have sex with men old enough to be my grandfather for a few hundred dollars a night.

No matter how much money I made, I spent it all. My real addiction to drugs began after I gave birth to my first child. I was seventeen. Marijuana and alcohol had been the extent of my drug use up to this point.

Then, I discovered cocaine. I started with snorting cocaine. Bo thought that snorting it was a "waste of good dope." So, he talked me into mainlining it, and I was hooked. We would shoot cocaine nonstop for days.

Once we started, we would keep on until all of our money was gone. We sold anything and everything that we could sell to keep on getting high. I spent two years of my life getting high day and night until I died. I mean, literally—I died.

I died in a sleazy hotel room on Dickerson Road. At the time, I was turning tricks for an escort service named "Charlie's Angels." The owner, "Charlie," found out that Bo and I liked to shoot cocaine and used us to "cop" the dope for him.

We had been shooting cocaine nonstop, eight-ball after eight-ball. I will never forget feeling the need to call and check on my child. I was so high that I wanted to keep on talking. I missed my daughter. I missed being a part of her life. Anne said she was asking about us because we hadn't stopped by for days.

As I sat there listening to Anne tell me about the cute things my daughter had done, Bo pulled up enough cocaine for both of us into one syringe. I got off the phone just in time to pump up my arm as Bo let me know he would pull the syringe out when he had given me my half. I watched as he methodically pushed the plunger all the way in, emptying my portion and his portion of the shot into my arm by mistake. That was all I remembered.

When my eyes rolled back in my head, and the convulsions started, he realized what he had done. Charlie frantically collected all of his drugs and ran out the door, leaving Bo to deal with my lifeless body lying on the hotel room bed.

Bo didn't know CPR, but he knew that my heart needed to beat again. He dragged me into the hotel bathtub and propped me up against the wall as he turned the shower on with frigid cold water. He took his fist and started punching me in my chest as hard as he could. After a while, I started to breathe again.

I didn't regain consciousness for some time. It was over an hour before I could speak. When I finally came around to the point that I could speak, I remember I was on the hotel room bed, soaking wet and numb. Bo stood over me, asking questions such as "What is your name?" But I couldn't think of my name, and I couldn't remember his name or where I was. Bo took me for a ride to get fresh air until I began to regain my memory. The first coherent sentence that I could muster was to ask for another shot of cocaine.

CHAPTER SIX

AN EMOTIONAL COMA

That night was a wake-up call. Bo was more shaken by my overdose than I was. We stopped shooting dope for a long time.

He let me take a break from prostituting, and we put an ad in the yellow pages to open a locksmith shop. Bo's dad had owned a local locksmith business for many years, but because of his constant drinking, the business had failed. During that time, Bo had learned the tricks of the trade from his dad and knew how to re-key locks, open locked cars, and cut keys for most vehicles. We went into business for ourselves.

We went back to drinking and smoking pot as our social entertainment. Within a few months, I was pregnant with our son. We had a semi-normal life. We rented a duplex and tried to be a family. We met with friends and played our guitars, drinking beer and singing country songs. But there were never any date nights or evenings at home with each other. He had to be on the go, playing poker, meeting his friends to drink, or shooting pool at the bar.

Still, there were the con-man schemes. Bo was always looking for a way to make it rich without working. He bought stolen items and resold them. Money was never put back into the business. We never had a checking or savings account, and bills didn't get paid regularly.

Some of our friends were making money by shoplifting and reselling the items, so I tried my hand at it. I stole specific items like sheet sets, telephones, or expensive jeans because people would give us orders of things they wanted. After being arrested for stealing a phone, I decided it wasn't worth it.

I gave birth to our son in May of 1989. Bo was there with a camera and held his son. He was so proud to have someone to "carry on the family name." The next day, he brought our daughter up to the hospital to meet her baby brother. He brought me a joint, and I snuck down to the bottom floor and got high behind the hospital.

Our lives were settled into a rhythm of drinking and making enough money to keep the rent paid until the day Anne cleaned out her safe. Let me explain. The year before I moved in, Anne's husband had died from cancer. Anne had hidden his medications in her safe all those years. I think she wanted to help us by giving us a bottle of Dilaudid because she knew they could be sold for a hefty price on the streets. But this sparked a whole new level of drug addiction.

A Vicious Cycle

Dilaudid is a highly addictive painkiller used to help people through the final months of a terminal illness. In Nashville, it was the drug second in demand next to cocaine. People who wanted a high similar to heroin could purchase half a pill for thirty dollars or a whole pill for fifty and be high the whole day.

But swallowing this pill was a waste of a good high. In order to get your money's worth, you had to shoot it. This took us back to the needle. We sold some of the pills but ended up buying cocaine to mix with it to create a speedball. By the time we ran out of the pills in our bottle, we had developed a new addiction.

To get more pills, we had to go to the projects and buy from the drug dealers who stood on the corners. Every day became a vicious cycle. We would spend all morning finding the first fifty dollars to get our "wake-up" high. We made a mad dash to the projects looking for someone who had a pill.

Sometimes, the police were so thick in the projects that I would drop Bo off a few blocks away, and he would walk up into the projects and meet me back in a nearby parking lot. Even though we knew that the police would impound the vehicle we were driving if we were arrested with drugs, we borrowed cars from his family and our friends to run our "little errand." They never knew where we were going.

If we made any more money through the night, we would get high again. The next day we would start the vicious cycle over again, searching for a "wake-up" high.

In drug addiction, I discovered nothing else matters except the next high. The reason I hated being addicted to cocaine is that there was never enough. No matter how much you had, you were never satisfied.

On cocaine, you would sell everything you could get your hands on for one more shot. But on Dilaudid, you would mellow out for a few hours, scratch your face, and nod.

During this time, we started "playing the doctors." We found out from our friends where we could go to get some prescriptions of Valium, Ativan, and Tylenol 4 with codeine. What we didn't take, we sold.

Between popping pills, shooting cocaine and Dilaudid, and smoking pot, you could probably guess where our money went. My mind was a fog of confusion, and my life was a wreck.

During a cocaine binge, we headed to the projects with twenty dollars to find some more coke. A group of drug dealers surrounded our car, trying to make a sell. While one guy put drugs in Bo's hand, another one grabbed our money. The guy with our money started running, but the dealer who put the drugs in Bo's hand wanted to get paid.

Bo panicked and stomped on the gas pedal, still holding on to the drugs. The dealer jumped in the window as our car pulled off. He repeatedly punched Bo in the head and wrestled with Bo as the car sped down the street.

As we topped a hill, we saw two police cars parked on the side of the street. Because we knew the police would chase us and we didn't know how to stop the drug dealer's attack, we pulled over. The dealer escaped into the woods, and we were left there to explain what had just happened.

In my purse were two very large bags of what looked like weed. It was real marijuana. It just wouldn't get the average dope smoker high. Bo called it "bunk" weed, and he sold it to unsuspecting truck drivers. The police searched our car, found the weed in my purse, and we went to jail. Our cocaine binge was ended for the night.

Uncomfortably Numb

Soon, I went back to another escort service to supply our habits and try to keep a roof over our heads. Anne was watching both of the kids now. Bo continued to answer any calls that came in for locksmith work.

We moved from place to place, sometimes living in motels for weeks at a time. Sometimes we slept on other people's couches. We rented a few rat-infested houses and a few rundown trailers during that time, but we never stayed anywhere for very long.

One night, I received a message from the escort office where I was working, telling me to call a certain number. They said that Bo had called and claimed that he was shot. I called immediately. Bo answered drunk and incoherent. He wouldn't tell me where he was or what had happened.

He just said, "Meet me at home. I've been shot." I went home and waited.

He showed up about eleven o'clock the next day. By then, I was frantic. Sure enough, he had been shot twice. One bullet had passed clean through the fleshy part of his side. The other bullet, he claimed to have taken out himself.

He wouldn't tell me where he had been or what he had done to get shot. He was wrapped tight with gauze, but he had not visited a hospital. I never found out what had happened.

The next day he received a call to re-key all of the locks in a huge house. I remember that Bo lost a lot of blood as he worked on that house. When we got paid for the job, I was stunned to see the name on the check. We had just re-keyed the locks in the house of a famous country music star while Bo was bleeding from a gunshot wound.

By this time, my heart was growing colder and harder toward Bo. I felt numb to the pain. We had fought many times, and I attempted to leave him a few times. But I was too afraid to actually leave town. He threatened that I would never see my kids again and swore to kill me if I found another man.

One time that I had succeeded in leaving him, he found me in the motel I had rented by the week. I took a handful of Valium as he walked in the door because I knew trouble was about to begin. He talked in a deceptively sweet voice as he looked through the room to see what I had been doing and if I was living there alone.

I was calm, very calm, and let him talk. My inner voice kept coaching me, saying, *Stay calm, and he won't hit you. Don't give him any reason to get mad.*

He found a knife over by the wet bar, a brand-new kitchen knife that was very sharp. He grabbed the knife as he slammed me against the wall, choking me. Laying the edge of the blade against my face and speaking through clenched teeth, he threatened to kill me.

I was so numb from the Valium and the misery of my life that I answered, "I don't care. I *really* don't care anymore." I stared into his eyes with no emotion. This was the first time that I had not tried to fight back. This was the first time that I didn't have a look of stark terror in my eyes or didn't beg him to stop. Actually, I was too mellow from the Valium to lift my arms and fight back.

He dropped the knife as the blood started to stream from an inch, long cut on my left cheek. Although the cut needed stitches, I just bandaged it and sat back down.

Suddenly, he was sorry. He began to apologize, asking me to come back to him. I just said, "Whatever." I had hit bottom. Something in me had snapped. I really didn't care.

Chapter Seven

Unspeakable Shame

I became pregnant again. This time I wasn't sure who the father of the baby was. I had been pressured a few times by different men to have sex without a condom. If the price was right or if they offered me drugs as an incentive, I gave in. Also, the condoms weren't always effective, and more than one had broken. My drug activity had interfered with my birth control pills, and now I was pregnant.

I found an abortion clinic and scheduled an appointment. I didn't tell Bo about my uncertainty, and he didn't ask why I wanted an abortion. I just told him that we couldn't handle another baby right now because we weren't raising the children that we had. He didn't care.

On the day of the procedure, we checked out of a cheap, weekly-rental motel. I was angry with myself for being such a weak woman. The only way I could deal with my guilt and shame was to turn it into anger. I answered him sharply, knowing that at any minute, he might slap my face, but I didn't care.

He drove me to the clinic that was located a few blocks away in an industrial park. There were very few signs on the white cinderblock building to advertise what really took place in there. He dropped me off at the abortion clinic like he was dropping me off at the mall without making any attempt to comfort or console me. He didn't ask me if I was going to be okay or whether I could do this alone. He just dropped me off and told me to call him at Anne's house when I was done. I kept reminding myself that I didn't care. It just fueled my anger more to think that I had to do this alone.

I filled out the paperwork and sat for a few minutes in the waiting room. A woman, dressed in scrubs and a white lab coat, took me into a room and handed me a Valium. I almost laughed in her face. One Valium wasn't going to help me!

I thought to myself, *Only one Valium. Are you kidding me?* It would take a lot more than that for me to escape the reality of what I was doing. I wanted to put a needle in my arm and make this whole thing disappear. I could crush that little fifty-dollar pill, mix it with warm water in the syringe, and leave all the shame, humiliation, and degradation behind. After one shot, I could face the world. But at that moment, all I had was one little Valium.

I consoled myself with the fact that I had just filled the Ativan prescription that I obtained from the doctor, and I wasn't selling them this time. I planned to use them *all*, keeping myself numb and free from reality for as long as possible. Along with the large bag of pot (and my plans to score a

Dilaudid), I felt that I could escape the pain. This conscious preparation was evidence that I knew that this was going to be the worst decision I had ever made.

I took the Valium and chewed it up so that it would quickly get into my bloodstream. The woman handed me a paper gown and led me to a room without any eye contact or verbal interaction. I changed into the paper gown and lay on the cold table, shivering and waiting.

My emotions went into a comatose state. *Nothing matters,* I told myself. That was how I had dealt with every bad decision that I had ever made. An emotional coma became my escape when I ran away from home, when I was abandoned on the mountain, and when I prostituted my body.

The days of watching someone else raise my children could only be endured by entering my emotional coma. It kept me from feeling the humiliation of having sex with men I didn't know for a handful of money that would be spent on drugs. This emotional coma came to my rescue again as an uncaring, faceless doctor came into the room, and I positioned my feet in the stirrups. From the time the doctor entered the room until the time he left was less than five minutes.

I felt the baby as it left my body. The doctor pulled the lifeless baby through what should have been a birth canal. Instead, it was a death canal.

At that moment, I realized I had killed my unborn child, and I was so ashamed. Suddenly I was aware that it wasn't just a fetus or a blob of tissue; it was my third child. Although I did not see my baby, I knew.

I have never forgotten that moment, nor have I forgotten that feeling of regret. There was no rewind button to reverse that moment. I realized too late that some choices you can't take back.

There was no one there to turn to and say, "What have I done!" Although the births of my other children were attended by the whole family, the death of my third child was a lonely event.

The doctor left the room as nonchalantly as he had entered just a few minutes before. I was left alone and empty. I felt more worthless than I had ever felt in my life.

I cried regretful tears and wiped them from my eyes. I dressed in my jeans and sweatshirt and looked into the mirror over the small sink in the bathroom. There was no makeup to hide my emptiness and self-loathing. I hated myself more than ever at that moment.

I sat in the waiting room for the required time to ensure that the bleeding was not excessive. I called Bo to come and pick me up. When he pulled up, he was already high. He never asked me how I was. He simply handed me a joint, and then he drove me to his mother's home in West Tennessee. I took a handful of Ativans. I just wanted to escape the guilt and shame.

His mother had a small trailer on a large piece of land in the middle of the country. We didn't tell her about the abortion. Bo just acted like we had come to stay for a while. I was depressed and didn't want to be there at all.

The country life didn't last long. We ran out of the pot supply and the prescriptions that we had carried with us. I had a fit and left with the kids in one of the cars that we had taken. I was halfway back to Nashville when the fuel gauge started showing empty. I pulled over and called Bo's mother. She said that he was right behind me. He caught up with us, fueled the car back up, and we came back to Nashville together.

I began living my life with a determined purpose. I was determined that I would never be sober another day in my life. I got high as a survival instinct because a sober day was not an option.

I became the walking dead. I walked through each day, lifeless on the inside. If I couldn't get high, I would get drunk, and I didn't even like to drink! But it was better than being sober enough to feel my shame, regret, and bitter self-hatred.

If I couldn't get drunk, I would drink a whole bottle of Nyquil. Sometimes, I had to steal the Nyquil because I was so desperate to forget the pain.

The Missing Weeks

At one of the lowest, most tumultuous moments in my life, I emptied another prescription bottle into my stomach. This time I almost succeeded in killing myself. It happened during a time when I was learning how to shoot cocaine without Bo's help. One day, I ventured alone into the projects and bought some cocaine that either had hallucinogens mixed with it, or I injected a stronger dose than I should have taken.

I had located a convenience store that had a bathroom located on the outside of the building, the kind you could lock from the inside. I mixed my drugs in a hurry and found a vein. The immediate rush began as usual but soon became something more than I expected. I went back out to the vehicle, with the cocaine rushing through my veins in full force and gaining momentum.

I began hallucinating as I drove, and I was very paranoid. I was driving our old van down and thought Bo and one of his friends were on the roof of the van, playing tricks on me. I kept stopping the van in the middle of the road, climbing out, and running around the van screaming at him to leave me alone. I was terrified that he would catch me doing drugs without him. At the same time, I was mad at him because he had been sending me to "work" at an escort service and getting high while I was gone.

Anyway, the tainted drugs mixed with my fear of him and anger at him made a volatile mixture. By the time I reached the apartment complex where we lived, I was convinced he was on the roof of the van. I could hear him laughing at me and taunting me. I saw beings that looked like aliens, leaning off the roof, peering in the windows, jeering at me. I assumed that they were really Bo and his friend, dressed up in costumes following me.

My rage boiled over as I pulled into the parking lot, and I rammed into his vehicle—a beautiful, royal blue Spyder convertible. I wasn't through. I backed the van up and punched the gas, smashing into his car over and over again.

I don't know if I parked the van or not. I remember walking into the apartment to find him sitting on the couch. Now, I was really scared. But he had no clue what was going through my mind. I went straight to the bathroom, grabbing a full prescription bottle with ninety Ativans from the vanity counter on my way. I swallowed all ninety pills and walked out into the living room. I threw the empty bottle at him and ran.

I ran into a wooded lot to escape and had to crawl on my hands and knees under bushes and through thick shrubs. I was terrified to be caught by him. I don't remember anything beyond crawling through the thick brush. That was the last clear memory I had for the next few weeks.

I was told that someone found me passed out in their driveway and called 9-1-1. An ambulance carried me to the emergency room, where the medical team pumped my stomach. Bo found me in the emergency room and smuggled me out because he knew that they would admit me to the psychiatric ward. A great deal of the prescription medication had absorbed into my system, and I became violent and hysterical, fighting and demanding that Bo let me go.

He let me get out of the car, and I went my own way. I only remember pieces of the next three weeks. I remember walking a long way in the dark, convinced that I could see Bo following me. I ended up being used by another pimp who was making me and another girl steal from the tricks. This guy kept me high and hid me in a miserable, rat-hole of a motel named Town Court.

News traveled back to Bo, and he came looking for me. He came packing his pistol and dragged me out of there. One of the first memories I had since the night I overdosed was of Bo kicking in the door with his pistol in hand. He came over to where I was huddled in the corner and asked me, "Are you ready to come home?"

The whole family had become concerned about my disappearance—Bo included. They were glad he had found me. We didn't talk much about the night I totaled his car. He did share the details of the parts I couldn't remember, but I never told him that I was secretly getting high that night.

Busted

Still, I was silently fuming about the gunshot and his secret activities. I knew there was more going on while I was working than I knew about. When I worked, he took all of my money to use on drugs. But he was getting high without me, and I wasn't getting any of it. As I began putting two and two together, I voiced my opinion.

He never admitted it. But he never denied my suspicions. So, I confronted him, "It is not fair that you are pulling robberies or stealing whatever you are stealing, and you don't give me any of the money or drugs. But you take my money and spend it how you want!"

His response was, "Fine, get in the car." He had been hanging out and getting high with a guy named Allen, who was outside in the driveway, waiting on Bo.

As we walked out and got in the car, Allen followed the directions that Bo gave him. We ended up at a convenience store. Bo climbed out of the passenger side and motioned for me to climb out of the back seat. I was still pouting and had my arms crossed as he told me what to do.

I thought *This was not what I meant! I meant he should share with me what he got, not make me do it with him!* I didn't want to rob a store.

We walked in together, and I just stood there glaring at him. He walked to the beer coolers, grabbed a twelve-pack of beer, and went to the counter. He looked down and saw a Doberman behind the counter next to the cashier and walked out of the store.

We got back into the car, and he told Allen which store to go to next. We ended up at a gas station closer to the projects. I stayed in the car this time. Bo approached the counter, pretending to have a gun in his pocket, and demanded the contents of the cash register. He came running out with under twenty dollars.

We headed to the projects for dope. On the way, he robbed another gas station. We ended up with less than fifty dollars. This wasn't what I wanted. I didn't want him to rob gas stations, and I didn't want either of us to go to prison!

We were arrested two blocks from the projects. The police pulled us out of the car and handcuffed us. Bo was charged with the robberies. Allen was offered a deal for testifying against us, which he took. The prosecutor charged me with two counts of attempted armed robbery, but I was released without bond.

Of course, Bo was charged with the robberies, and his bail was high. Although his family wanted to post his bond, they didn't have enough cash available. Bo asked me to go back to the streets prostituting until I could get enough money to post his bond.

It took me a while because I was using some of the money along the way to get high. He kept calling his grandmother's house from the jail, wondering what was taking me so long to get the money together. I finally had enough, and he was released on bond until our court date.

We took a bus down to West Tennessee, where his mother was still living. He was planning for us to escape to Canada, a decision that would mean separation from my children forever. I would have to take on a new identity and live like my children never existed. I cried bitter tears as we traveled down toward Jackson.

CHAPTER EIGHT

LEFT ALONE

Have I mentioned the fact that I loved Bo? As messed up as he was, in his own sick, twisted way, he loved me. In my own sick and twisted way, I loved him too.

My mom later told me, "Michelle, I knew that you were just as addicted to Bo as you were to drugs. I knew you'd never stop without him." She was right. I couldn't live with him, and I couldn't live without him. Just like hundreds of other women who get beaten and mistreated, yet they stay with the one who hurts them, I was convinced that I couldn't make it without him.

I was relieved when Bo gave up on the idea of running away to Canada. I was surprised when he started preparing himself to do his time. Our time back in the countryside was long enough for Bo to put some things in perspective. He decided to come back and face his sentence.

When he came back, he talked to the prosecutors to plea bargain for my charges to be dropped. If he went through with it, I would walk, and he would serve eight to ten years in the state penitentiary. I wasn't sure what to think.

During the time that we were waiting for the sentencing, we still fought. He was ready for this great turnaround. He wanted me to get a regular job after he went in and quit doing drugs. He wanted me to live with his grandmother and raise our children.

All of these things would have been exactly what I was hoping to hear six or seven years ago. But, after years of selling my soul, I didn't think I could be normal again. After years of medicating my shame with a syringe, I didn't know if I could escape.

Of course, he still wanted me to "work" right now because we needed money for the lawyer. After I got off work at the escort service, I started going by the bar where a guy who had cocaine would supply me. I went after hours when the bar was closed, but the guy was the owner and lived in the back. I was paranoid about Bo catching me, but my need for the needle drove me to do it. After a few hours there, I would catch a cab back to Bo's grandmother's house, where we were living until our trial.

After a disagreement, I didn't come back for about four days. I worked at the service at night and went to different places during the day. His mother called the escort service with an urgent message that I call her. I called in between tricks to find out what she wanted.

She begged me to come back to Bo. She told me that he loved me and was sorry for the way our lives had turned out.

She said he was a mess without me and really needed me. It was all the things I wanted to hear him say, not his mother. I waited until the next day. But I went back.

His attitude was different. I quit working and stayed around with the kids and the rest of the family as we waited to appear in court.

Our court date was scheduled for a Monday morning. Bo promised Anne that he would go to church with her on Sunday. That Sunday morning, Anne took the kids and went to church like she did every Sunday. Bo woke up late and scrambled around to get ready. Although they had already left, Bo kept his word and followed Anne to church, arriving after the service had started.

I was shocked that he would really go. He tried to convince me that I needed to go too. I told him he was out of his mind! I went through all of the excuses about the walls caving in and lightning striking the building. I didn't go. I stayed at the house by myself.

When they all came bouncing in the house after church, they were thrilled and excited. The kids were jumping up and down, and Anne was smiling ear to ear. Even Bo was unusually happy for someone who was facing ten years of prison time.

Anne announced to me that Bo had gotten saved. I wasn't sure what that meant so, they explained to me that Bo had went up to have the pastor pray for him and had asked Jesus to save him. I still didn't know why that was such a big deal.

A man from the church who had prayed with Bo at the altar that day had given Bo a cassette tape with some Christian music. Bo really enjoyed it and listened to it throughout the day. He asked me to read the Bible to him since he couldn't read very well. I rolled my eyes but started reading. I wasn't impressed with all of this Bible stuff and church songs.

Sentencing Day

The next day, we faced the music. As we walked into the courthouse, we were all a bundle of nerves. The whole family stood in the hallway, waiting for our place on the docket, when one of Bo's friends came walking toward us. I thought that it was really nice of him to come to show us that support.

I turned around to say something to Anne. When I turned back, Bo and his friend had disappeared! Fifteen minutes later, Bo returned. He said they had gone to the bathroom. In reality, he had gone to a bathroom on another floor. because his friend wanted to "help him out." None of us were aware that his friend had placed a morphine patch on his side.

The morphine patch was the size of a piece of notebook paper and worked like a nicotine patch works. It was something experimental, being used on cancer patients in their last stages of the disease. His friend thought they would probably take Bo into custody, and this patch would keep him high for the first few days of processing. It had enough morphine to time-release over three days.

They sentenced Bo and accepted the plea bargain. The judge announced that he had a number of days to put his affairs in order since he was out on bond. We left the courtroom, relieved that we had a few more days before he had to report to intake.

By the time we left, Bo was beginning to feel the effects of the morphine. He still hadn't told me about it. He let me in on his secret that evening as he was nodding out in mid-sentence, unable to stay awake.

The only drug that I had indulged in for weeks was pot. Bo offered to cut the patch in half and put half of it on me. I tried to convince him to pull it off and let me wear it for a few hours. But he wanted to keep the high he had going. So, he cut off half of the patch and gave one side of it to me.

I never felt a thing. I waited for the least little feeling, but there was nothing. I finally resolved that I could go the next day and get something for myself since it was too late to do anything that night.

So, Bo enjoyed the Christian music and made me read the Bible to him some more. He went to bed and slept hard through the night. In the morning, he was still sleeping hard. I had to climb over him to get out of the bed, and I didn't even wake him up. That was unusual. He was a light sleeper. And for a man who didn't snore, he was snoring loudly. I assumed it was the morphine making him sleep harder than usual.

I got myself dressed for the day and helped Anne with the kids. I was ready to go get something to get high, so I kept trying to wake him up by making noise in the room. I was willing to put up with him being angry with me if it meant he would help me get to the projects.

I let our four-year-old son wander into the room with his out-of-tune guitar and began to "play" while he shouted the words to *Rocky Top* at the top of his lungs. I started the vacuum cleaner and vacuumed the floors in every other room and ended in the room where he slept. Finally, I switched the vacuum off and turned around to wake him up.

Bo wasn't even breathing. I called his name and shook him. Still, he wasn't breathing. Our son was on the floor with the guitar, singing his song. Anne was in another part of the house. I began screaming for her to call an ambulance. The fire station was at the end of the street. They could be there quickly.

I tried to remember everything I had ever heard about CPR. I tried to breathe into his mouth, but the air I pushed in with my breath just came bubbling back out of his mouth into my mouth. It didn't even seem to enter his lungs.

I tried to stand over him and push on his chest. The bed was so soft that his whole body just sunk into the mattress. So, I tried to pull him onto the floor. His head hit the nightstand, and his body was tangled up in the sheets. He was covered in sweat, and I couldn't get a good grip. I started to cry in desperation and began saying to him. "Don't you die, Bo!"

Within minutes the paramedics rushed in and moved me out of the way. They pulled Bo's lifeless body out of the tangled sheets and onto the floor. As two men began CPR, another brought in a stretcher.

Anne pulled the kids into the back room and called down the street where Bo's sister and Mom were. They pulled up in front of the house as Bo's body was being lifted into the ambulance with the paramedics still working to revive him.

I climbed into the front seat, and the ambulance sped toward the hospital that was about eight minutes away. I answered the questions that the paramedics asked, trying to explain about the morphine and the time-released patch.

The hospital staff escorted me to a private waiting room. As Bo's family arrived, they brought them to this private room. I tried to explain the morphine and the time-released patch to the family because everyone wanted to know what had happened. We tried to reassure each other that everything would be okay. We assumed that they would revive him, and everything would be fine.

Then, a woman counselor from the hospital arrived to talk with us. Slowly, we began to realize that his condition was more serious than we thought, and the hospital was sending us someone to help us if he died. The medical team finally came to the family waiting room to tell us they had been able to restore a heartbeat. I will never forget the look on Bo's mother's face as she asked the question that we all were afraid to ask. "So, isn't everything okay now that you have resuscitated him?"

They explained that Bo was being kept alive by the machines that were breathing for him. The morphine patch had released three days of morphine into his body in one day. Bo had been without sufficient oxygen throughout the night because his diaphragm was unable to expand adequately. The noise that I mistook for snoring was Bo struggling to breathe! I had been selfishly thinking about getting high while he was struggling to hang on to life.

We were moved up to the intensive care waiting room. Bo was only living because of the machines that kept his body alive. We were allowed to go into the room with Bo a few times a day for a few hours.

Family members and people from Anne's church came to visit us. Soon, our friends heard about it and came to the hospital. Some people thought Bo had tried to commit suicide to avoid going to prison. Regardless of their suspicions, everyone was in a state of shock.

High in the Hospital

Some of our friends came up to the hospital and brought me something to help me cope. One girl took me into the bathroom and gave me a Dilaudid and a syringe. I felt guilty as I took my place back in the waiting room next to Bo's family as the drug took effect.

But the guilt was short-lived. My friend came every day and helped me out. I kept the syringe in my shoe, and when the guy from the bar called and asked me if I needed anything, I asked him to bring me some cocaine so that I could stay awake.

Bo's condition had not improved. As a matter of fact, his brain was swelling. You could visibly see the area around his temples and his eyes protruding. The doctor called the immediate members of the family together for a meeting. He explained that Bo was brain dead and had suffered so much brain damage that he would be a vegetable for the rest of his life. He gave us the option to unplug the machines and let him pass away or keep him plugged up to the machines indefinitely in a coma.

It was during this time that the man from Anne's church who had prayed with Bo at the altar and given him the cassette of Christian music came to the hospital. I had never met him before, and he wasn't what I expected to see from the church. He was wearing a black leather biker's vest and wore a long ponytail down his back. His face was covered in a thick beard, and he carried a huge, worn, black Bible. He said that he wanted to pray for Bo because he believed that God would heal him.

I didn't think his prayer would do any good. Still, I asked Bo's mother if she cared that this man prayed for Bo. She didn't seem too keen on the idea either. It sounded far out to both of us, but we took him to Bo's cubicle in ICU. We let him pray, and he prayed with all of his might. Personally, I was caught between feeling uncomfortable and feeling sorry for this guy.

He went back to the waiting room with us and began to talk to me about my life. I skirted around as many questions as I could, until finally, he suggested that we go to the chapel and talk.

I didn't want to go to the chapel, and I didn't want to talk. This man was insistent. He kept on until I agreed to go. As we walked out of the waiting room, my friend from the bar was walking up the hall. I tried to get out of the chapel meeting, but the preacher said he would wait. I walked to the other end of the hall with the friend from the bar who slipped me a twenty-cent piece (twenty dollars' worth) of cocaine.

What a mess! My husband was being kept alive by machines. The doctors said there was no hope. Some biker/preacher wanted to pray with me in the chapel. I had a syringe in my shoe and cocaine in my pocket. I repeat—what a mess!

I went to the chapel and listened to the preacher. Well, I was halfway listening. He was insistent and continued to ask questions that made me think. He was determined to get through to me.

At first, I heard his dialogue as "religious stories" about Jesus coming to the earth so that He could die for my sins. But the more the man explained, the more it became real to me. This story began to take on life and become personal to me.

I thought to myself, *Really? Do you mean that God doesn't hate me? Is it true that God would help me?* When the man asked me to pray with him, that one glimmer of hope was present in my heart. *If God would really help me, I need help.*

I prayed his prayer, repeating the words of repentance. I didn't feel any different. I didn't have that silly smile on my face that Bo was wearing the day he had come home from church. I wasn't aware of any change. I said "goodbye" to the preacher in the hallway.

Next, I did what any junkie would do. I went to the bathroom downstairs in the emergency room waiting area. I locked the door. I mixed up the cocaine in the cap of my syringe. I searched in the dimness of the bathroom light for a vein and pushed in the plunger.

I waited for the trains, the sound of the blood rushing past your eardrums as the cocaine accelerates your heart. There was nothing. I felt absolutely nothing. Maybe, God heard my prayer and was holding me to my words of commitment. I cleaned up and returned to the waiting room.

I was too high on these different drugs to show any authentic emotion. It is no wonder that Bo's family was distancing themselves from me. It is no surprise that Bo's mom started thinking that I had something to do with him dying. I can't remember if I cried. I don't know if I looked sad. I was numb. My memories of this time are sketchy and focused on drugs. It is as if I wasn't there for half of this nightmare.

When we turned off the machines, the family was gathered together in the room. I remember the moment, but I can't remember showing any emotion. When the machine ceased breathing for Bo, it was the last breath he took. I'm not sure how long we sat in that room saying our goodbyes.

I remember that I was the last to leave. I sat next to his body, trying to grasp the fact that those eyes would never open again. I lifted the sheet that was draped over his body and tried to memorize every scar and every tattoo. I held his hand and whispered, "What do you want me to do now, Bo? Just tell me what to do."

Chapter Nine

MY NEXT OVERDOSE

U p until this point, I only thought that my life was out of control. After Bo's death, my life had absolutely no direction. Bo had been the voice that told me what to do and how to get it done.

All of the animosity that I felt over the years was really masking the fact that I had no life outside of him. I didn't know how to think for myself or take care of myself. I was so lost.

Would you think I was crazy if I told you I don't know what I did that night after Bo left this world? I don't know if I went home with his family or if I went to get high. I really don't remember. I don't remember telling my children that their father was gone.

My daughter remembered that her grandmother, aunt, and I sat them down in a circle and tried to explain that their daddy would never come back. I don't know how long my children cried or who wiped away their tears.

The next memory that I have was in the funeral home. I thought to myself, *I can't take this. I can't make it through this unless I get something to help me.* I placed a call from the funeral home to the doctor who prescribed the Ativan, and he called in a prescription for me. The same girl who had visited me in the hospital showed up with a Dilaudid, and I shot up in the funeral home restroom.

Someone brought the children to the funeral home, and we took them in to see Bo's body. This is the first time I can remember seeing how my children were taking the loss of their father. I was so selfish and focused on how this was affecting my life that I wasn't thinking about helping my children or anyone else in the family through this moment.

Our daughter had always been a "daddy's girl." She was six years old and very grown-up. While her brother was too young to comprehend the brevity of the moment, she was old enough to understand that daddy wasn't coming back. When she approached the casket, she reached to touch Bo's face and began to scream in anger, "That is not my daddy! You're lying! That is not him!"

The funeral director closed the sliding partition to stop anyone else from entering the viewing area as the whole family stood there in shock. I pulled her hand away as she was hitting Bo's face and smearing the makeup that had been applied by the undertaker who had prepared his body.

Gently, the funeral director suggested that everyone step out and they would fix the damage. We tried to explain that this was her daddy's body, but she loudly refused to accept. Someone took the kids back home, and I don't remember seeing them again for a few days.

I wish that someone would have shaken me, screamed at me, and told me to get a grip on reality. Why didn't someone stop me?

Instead, the family began to resent me. When I walked into the room where all of the family was gathered, I felt cold stares and heard faint whispers. I can't blame them. I was stoned and drugged out during my husband's wake, and things got worse on the day of the funeral service.

The funeral home was packed. The word had spread far and wide about Bo's death, and many people had come to pay their last respects. We were all dressed in our best black apparel. I had a black skirt and my high-heeled, black leather boots.

Word was brought to me that Allen had shown up. I was furious and went marching through the funeral home to find him. You could hear me screaming. "Where is he? How dare he show his face here?" When I found him, he very respectfully apologized and began to share his condolences. But I was fit to be tied!

I lit into him, scratching, clawing, and kicking like a banshee! He calmly said, "I understand. I'll go. I'm sorry. I don't want to cause trouble." That didn't change anything. As he walked out of the building and to his car, I kicked him in his rear end every step of the way. I broke the heel off of my right boot. That poor guy!

When he drove off, the director of the funeral home approached me and said, "If you don't get control of yourself, you are going to have to leave. We need to get started."

I squared my shoulders, looked him in the eyes, and said, "I'm ready to start." On the way back into the funeral home, I picked up the broken heel of my boot and found my seat.

After the funeral, I went to score another Dilaudid. When I went back to Anne's house, all of the flowers from the funeral were on her front porch. I went inside, but everything felt different. I didn't feel like I belonged there anymore. I didn't want to sleep in the bed where Bo had died. I didn't know what to say to anybody. When they asked me, "What are you going to do?" I couldn't answer.

The only thing I had done for the past eight years on a consistent basis was to get high. I didn't know any other pattern of life. I had never made any plans for my life beyond tomorrow. I wasn't a good mother. I was a prostitute and a junkie. So, I did the only thing I knew how to do. I kept getting high.

My life was chaos. I didn't know where I was half of the time. I tried to go to the places that we used to go and realized that those were his friends. They weren't my friends. I didn't fit in there without him.

I was so alone with nowhere to turn. I didn't talk to my mother. I hadn't spoken to my father since we left Florida with his money. I hadn't spoken to my brother since I ran away from home. I had no relationship with my children.

The only family that I had known for the last eight years was Bo's family, and I had ruined that as well.

Anne asked me to sign the life insurance policy that she was taking out on me. She had kept a small life insurance policy on Bo that had covered his funeral expenses. I didn't want to leave anyone with the burden of burying me if I died, so I gladly signed it. At the same time, she convinced me to sign custody of the children over to her. I agreed with her; it would probably be best.

I went to the bar owned by the guy who had supplied me with coke in the hospital. Eventually, I stayed there every night. He continued to provide me with plenty of cocaine and gave me money to buy some Dilaudid, too.

It was in the back of this bar that I died. I had been doing cocaine for three days and nights nonstop. I hadn't eaten or had anything to drink for days. It was midmorning on a Sunday, and the bar hardly had any customers. I begged for more cocaine and convinced him to make it a bigger piece because I wasn't "feeling" it. That should have been a signal. But junkies don't think rationally.

My teeth were grinding together. My jaw was twitching as I sprinkled the precious white powder into the cap of the syringe. I pulled up just the right amount of water and added it to the powder in the cap. I pulled the liquid cocaine into the syringe and tapped the air to the top.

The sounds of the Sunday afternoon customers in the bar where I was secretly shooting dope were soon drowned out by the anticipated sound of the trains that came thundering through my head as my heart answered the call of the cocaine by pumping blood through my body at an outrageous pace.

Added to the strong dose of cocaine was the fact that I had been shooting nonstop since Friday night. Perhaps, that is why I slipped out of consciousness before I could even untie the belt from my left arm. It could be why my heart stopped beating, and my breath left my body.

As I died, it was different than the numbness I had felt in my first cocaine overdose. I was aware of my surroundings. Life and death had never seemed so real, so vivid. I was very afraid.

Darkness surrounded me. Suddenly, I stood in front of a skull. It was not a whole skeleton. It was a giant skull that was as tall as I was. Hands reached from the darkness, trying to pull me into death. At that moment, I was aware of the reality of death. I wasn't ready to die, and I didn't want to be pulled into the darkness.

I turned and ran with all of my might. I ran back to my body. When I reached my body, I kept running. The man performing CPR on me was shocked. One minute he was pumping my chest, desperately trying to bring me back to life. The next minute, he found himself fighting a frantic, panicked, half-crazed girl. I fought as if those hands were still reaching for me.

I ran from the back room of the bar and down the streets of the inner city before I slowed down. With blood dripping from my arm and a cold rain pelting my face, I realized that hell was a real place, and I didn't want to go there.

Before this moment in my life, I didn't care about dying. I felt as if I was living in hell on earth. I didn't think that heaven was a possibility for me. I didn't know that God would forgive me of my sins. When the man who came to the hospital had explained salvation to me in the chapel that night, it was the first time that I had heard the truth about God in a way that I could understand it.

When I had attended church with my grandparents, I never grasped the concept that everyone has sinned and needs the forgiveness that Jesus' blood can provide. When I went to church with my friend, I didn't hear the plan of salvation. I had fun and sang songs but never grasped the truth about God.

I went back to Anne's house and told her what had happened. I don't think she took me seriously. By now, they were kind of put out with me.

I went to the evening service at the church where Bo had gotten saved. I sat on the front row, waiting for the sermon to be over. When he opened for prayer, I jumped up to talk to him. He asked me why I needed prayer, and I answered, "I died today and went to hell. I need help."

They prayed a prayer for me, and as quick as it started, it was over. I walked into the parking lot disappointed that I didn't have any direction.

I decided that I needed to get off of drugs and found out about a government program through my friends. This program supplied methadone to help you get off of heroin or Dilaudid. The only catch to this program was that I had to travel to Chattanooga every day for two or three weeks to pick up the methadone.

My friends were carpooling down together. We had to meet early in the morning and drive to Chattanooga to be there when the clinic opened.

Methadone messed me up! I totaled three cars and don't remember where I left them. I passed out naked in someone's house and was draped across a chair when his parents and his three-year-old son came in. But I was trying to clean myself up!

I bought a Bible. It cost me a quarter at the thrift store. I tried to read it because I wanted God's help. Usually, I nodded off after just a few minutes of reading. But I would wake up and try to read again. I sat there with that Bible, nodding for hours, and never successfully read the pages.

The wife of the man who had visited the hospital had dropped by Anne's house to leave her phone number for me. She invited me to attend a revival taking place in another church.

I didn't know what a "revival" was, but I agreed to go. I was high on the methadone treatment and nodded through the first service. Although I don't remember what happened that night, I was told that I had a conversation with the preacher's wife. Evidently, I cussed her out when she was trying to pray for me. I don't remember that at all! I was so high with the heavy doses of methadone and slept through church.

The couple offered to let me stay with them for a while under certain conditions. I couldn't tell anyone where I was, and I couldn't bring anyone over to the house. I agreed to their conditions and slept on their couch. I discovered later that they stayed up throughout the night praying over me to be free from the addiction.

I went back to the revival with them the next night and, once again, fell asleep during the sermon. This time the preacher came to where I was seated and woke me up. He said, "Do you really want help, girl?"

For that one moment, it seemed as if I was in my right mind. I stood to my feet and answered him. "Yes, sir. I do."

He reached out to pray for me, and I fell to the floor. I'm not sure how long I was there, but when I got to my feet, I whispered to the woman seated next to me, "I think that man knocked me down. Did you see him knock me down?"

Suddenly, I realized that I was sober and clear-headed, more than I had been in eight years. My mind was alert, and I could actually think clearly. Although I had prayed in the hospital chapel months before, I had not really surrendered my life to Jesus Christ as my Lord and Savior. I gave my life to God that night, August 10th, 1992.

CHAPTER TEN

LIFE LESSONS

I am not sure that I had ever been in "my right mind" before this point in my life. Before the addiction, the prostitution, the abuse, the shame, and the failures, I wasn't really in a "right mind." Now, I could face my life with the ability to make right choices. My perception was free of the despair that had enslaved me, and I saw hope for my future. That evening, I flushed my marijuana, methadone, and Ativan down the drain.

The revival at the church was going on every night, so I took my Bible and followed along with the preachers, soaking up God's Word like a sponge. I learned so much, and I had so much that I needed to learn.

The couple who had taken me into their home was so patient with me. Not only was I clueless about the things of God and the Bible, but I also didn't know how to shop for groceries, clean house, pay bills, or get up before noon. I had to learn everything about being responsible!

My lessons started right away as they took me to put in applications for a job. I had not worked a regular job since I was sixteen years of age, and being a waitress was the only job experience I had. I found a job at a restaurant near the mall. Since I didn't have any money, they helped me buy the necessary clothes for my uniform and gave me a ride to work every day.

My next lesson in responsibility was my car. The car I had been driving was not legal. I had bought the car on payments from an individual who I had met under illegal circumstances. He disappeared, and I had no title. Some people from the church tried to help me search for the title so that I could locate the owner. The vehicle registration number came back as stolen. I had been driving a stolen car! Needless to say, I couldn't drive it anymore.

I set up a meeting with Bo's family and invited my mom and stepdad to attend. My friends from church went with me to share the great news of my freedom. My enthusiasm about the great transformation in my life was not reciprocated by any member of the family. I told them that I was clean, had a job, and wanted to raise my kids. I thought that they would be pleased and would want my kids to have a regular home with their mother.

But they had no intention of returning the custody of my children to me because they didn't expect my transformation to last. After that meeting, they didn't have civil conversations with me for quite some time. Although I was disappointed by their response, I understood. They had watched me self-destruct for the last eight years, never making any responsible decisions.

New Responses

My previous method of responding when things got tough was to quit or run. But I wasn't who I used to be. I wasn't the messed-up failure anymore. My mind was changed by the truths I was learning from God's instruction manual. I faced this mess I had made with hope and a lot of encouragement and prayer from the people in the church.

I went to the courts to find out what it would take to get custody of my children returned to me. On the day of the hearing, Anne's attorney pointed out to the judge my long history of addiction, my arrest record, my lack of a legal driver's license, and my lack of a home. They even brought a group of people to testify about my crimes and drug use.

The judge shocked us all by her stern response, "I'm not interested in what Michelle did in the past. I want to know what Michelle is doing right now." Right then, I knew that God was on my side. I walked into that courtroom hoping for God's mercy, and I knew I had just witnessed the favor of God.

The judge appointed me an attorney who acted as a mediator to review my case and set up supervised visitation at Anne's house. The mediator explained what the judge would want me to accomplish to show that I was ready and able to take care of my children. This included having a home suitable for the children and me, having a legal driver's license, passing required drug screenings, and having a consistent work record.

This long list of requirements seemed like a lot for a person as irresponsible as I had been. I am sure that Bo's family didn't think I could pull it off, but I was willing to do my part. I also believed that God wanted me to have my children and would help me by doing the things that I was incapable of doing.

I began researching what it would take to get my driver's license back. I discovered that I had nearly two thousand dollars in fines and tickets. Also, there was a judgment against me from a car wreck in which I was uninsured. The amount of the judgment was nearly three thousand dollars. In addition to the fines and the judgment, there was a fee of almost one thousand dollars required to reinstate my license.

This looked impossible, and it was just the first step in a long list of things I had to do! I hung up the phone after gathering all of the information, and my heart began to sink. I didn't make enough money as a waitress to pay for all of these fines and fees and still get an apartment before the court's deadline.

I put a coin in the payphone and called the pastor from the church. I didn't want to open my mouth and ruin everything I had prayed by telling her how I felt and what my circumstance looked like. I simply said, "Please speak some faith to me."

She began declaring God's report. "My God shall supply all your need according to His riches in glory. God owns the cattle on a thousand hills. You are the head and not the tail." She unleashed Scripture after Scripture for the next few minutes until I was convinced of God's faithfulness and my victory. I was in a faith fight, and I was fighting for my children for the first time in my life.

To my surprise, my court-appointed attorney was able to get the judgment reduced and had most of the fines and tickets erased. I rejoiced and shouted all over the place. God's favor was working on my behalf!

I experienced supernatural favor even more as people from the church and at my job began giving me money to help. More than once, I received a hundred-dollar bill as a tip. It took a few months, but I was able to obtain my driver's license before the next court appearance.

During this time, I was granted scheduled, supervised visits with my children. But at my first visit, Anne turned me away for being five minutes late.

The people I was living with were so helpful to drive me everywhere. They picked me up from work on one side of town, and we rushed across town in the middle of afternoon traffic. We arrived at Anne's house five minutes past the time that the court-ordered visit was supposed to begin.

When I went to the door, Anne barely opened the door. She informed me that since I was late, she wasn't going to let me have the visit. My little boy saw me through the crack in the door and came running to hug me. Anne pushed him behind her and told him, "No, you can't see her." She shut the door in my face and left me with tears running down my face.

I have to admit that I was confused by her behavior. When Bo was alive, we took the kids whenever we wanted and kept them as long as we wanted. During that time, everybody knew we were either drinking or getting high.

Now, I was living clean and sober, actually working a job, and trying to live a normal life. But she wouldn't even let me in the house. I didn't argue. The next day I called my attorney who contacted Anne's lawyer. I made sure that I was early for the next visit.

Anne never made the visits comfortable. She didn't speak to me or look me in the eye. Her house was always full of other hostile family members who glared at me as I walked in and as I walked out.

When I came for the visit, I was escorted back to a small room that doubled as the laundry and toy room. I was in that little room for four hours a week, playing with my children. I learned how to play with them. I had to keep their attention because if they got bored, they went to another part of the house where I wasn't allowed. I probably spent more quality time with my kids during those visits than ever before.

Years later, Anne told me that she was testing me. She wanted to see how bad I really wanted my kids. She surely put me to the test and made me walk the line, but I am glad for it today. I discovered how valuable my relationship with my children really was. I found out that being a good mother required that I become unselfish. I had to put their stability and security above my needs or feelings.

By the time I returned for the custody hearing, I had passed every random drug test, obtained my legal driver's license, received a reference from my employer for steady work, and moved into a two-bedroom apartment. None of these things happened in the blink of an eye. But God's favor was apparent in each step I took. The apartment was rented the day before I was scheduled for the social worker's inspection. The people from my church brought furniture, dishes, towels, and toys. Within twenty-four hours, I went from sleeping on someone's couch with minimal belongings to having my own fully furnished apartment. I had beds, a couch, and even pictures on my wall! When I appeared before the judge for the final custody hearing, I was granted custody of my children with no hesitation.

Learning to Walk with God

Step by step, God began to establish my life. The Word of God became real to me as I sat in church, listening to the preaching, and following along in my Bible. I had so much to learn about God, and I desired to do things His way.

Knowing the will of God was very important to me. I did not want to make the wrong choices that would lead my life back to destruction. I discovered God's Word contains His will. If I prayed in line with the Word of God, I was praying in line with His will. If I lived in accordance with what is in His Word, I was living in line with His will. Whenever I learned something from the Bible, I would adjust my life to fit what God said.

When I began to pray for a husband, I went to the Word of God to get the details of what to pray. I asked God for a man who was stronger and more knowledgeable than I was in the Word of God, a man who would love my children like his own, and a man who would praise and worship God without reservation.

There were a couple of guys in the church who were interested in dating me. But they didn't qualify according to my prayer list. I wanted God's will for my life, and I wasn't interested in wasting time on anyone who wasn't in line with what I asked for in prayer.

When I met Philip Steele, I heard God speak to my heart that if I was willing to believe, I could have Philip as my husband. I shook my head and thought, *Is that just me, or was that really you, God?* I felt that reassurance again in my heart.

I hid this in my heart, praying and searching for God's perfect will for my life. As I was shaking hands with Philip on the front stairs of the church, I asked him, "Did you know that you are my miracle?" Each time that we met, our handshakes were long, and our eye contact spoke words that we couldn't say.

My faith and patience were rewarded when I became Mrs. Philip Steele almost a year later. We never dated before our wedding because we wanted our marriage built on integrity and God's righteousness. Other than phone conversations and long handshakes in the church, we stayed apart.

Philip truly is the man of my dreams. His walk with God is an ongoing inspiration to me. He is a strong, devoted husband and father, with God's call clearly on his life. Philip Steele is everything I asked for and much more.

Sabotaged by Shame

In the first year of our marriage, I discovered I was pregnant. We were expecting our first child together! This time things were so different in my life. There were no drugs or alcohol. I could enjoy and share this experience with Philip. I could enjoy bringing a new life into the world, a life that represented our love.

Philip and I didn't care what other people thought about the fact that we were going to have another child to add to our ready-made family. We started planning, spending hours discussing different name choices, and wondering if we would have a boy or a girl. We shared the news with the children to prepare them for their new baby brother or sister. Our life was picture-perfect.

Then, one day, I noticed a faint flow of blood. When I mentioned it to my sister-in-law, her face took on an expression of horror. Since I hadn't seen a doctor yet for prenatal care, she made an emergency appointment for me at a doctor's office. Philip was at work when I called to tell him that I was on my way to the doctor's office. I stopped by his job on the way, and Philip and I prayed together. Philip was so positive, encouraging me to think the best.

On the way to the doctor's office, a sense of shame, lying dormant in my subconscious mind, began to awaken. In the back of my mind, I began to hear a thought that didn't originate from my time reading God's Word. It didn't originate from the teaching of my pastors. It wasn't a thought that agreed with anything in my new Christian life. It was a haunting thought that had been buried for years in my mind, waiting for the perfect moment to sabotage my faith when I needed it the most.

I thought about the abortion from my past, and the shame came flooding into my heart. The thoughts began to bombard my mind, *I am going to lose this baby because I killed my last child. I don't deserve to have this baby because I didn't value the life of my last child. I am reaping what I sowed.*

I wasn't spiritually aware of the fact that those thoughts were attacks of the enemy. I didn't realize I needed to cast down those imaginations and raise the shield of faith. I didn't know how to declare God's Word or access the power of Jesus' blood to help me deal with the shame. Shame robbed my faith of the strength necessary to receive from God. I placed my shield of faith to the side and began to weep with empty, shame-filled tears from my past.

The doctor searched for a heartbeat but to no avail. As he pointed out the form of my lifeless child on the screen of the ultrasound machine, those empty, haunting tears from my past wandered down my face. Shame gave way to grief and sorrow as I realized my child was dead.

In a miscarriage, there is no funeral or casket. People act like you are overreacting because the baby wasn't fully formed or ready to be born. But the grief is just as real. The loss of a life is just as real. It can be so confusing because people expect the parents to just forget about this loss, but I couldn't just forget. Miscarriage is the death of a child you love. My baby had a name. My baby already had a place in my heart, but I would never get to hold him in my arms.

I was outraged by the things some people said to console us. For example, "God allowed this because He knows what is best," or "We can't explain why God did this." None of their words offered comfort or peace. Even knowing that my baby was in heaven with God didn't ease the pain of loss or the weight of the shame.

Philip wanted answers and embarked on a spiritual search. Philip refused to accept their statements at face value, so he prayed and searched God's Word. He came into our room one morning after time in prayer and took me gently by my hands. He said, "I can't explain why this happened, but I know it was not God's fault. Jesus gives life and abundant life. The enemy is the one responsible for killing, stealing, and destroying (John 10:10). We were attacked by the devil, and we lost that fight. But it won't happen again! We are going to trust God and shut any door to the enemy." We prayed together and resolved that we wouldn't lose another battle.

A Firmer Foundation

Philip and I followed God's plan for our lives, moving our family from Hendersonville, Tennessee, to Kansas City, Missouri, in the process. Within the year after moving to Kansas City, I became pregnant again. This time, we had a firmer foundation of the Word of God established in our hearts. My husband laid his hands on my swollen stomach and declared God's Word over our child. We arrested every thought that tried to provoke fear and praised God for His hand upon our baby.

Our foundation of faith was put to the test the day our daughter was born. We were experiencing great joy in the moments after she was born, celebrating and calling family to tell them the good news. I waited for the nurse to bring her back and place her in my arms. Instead, the nurses were exchanging looks of concern as they placed an oxygen mask over her face. Whenever the mask was removed, my daughter's body began to turn blue.

The medical team removed our baby from the room to investigate the problem. The next twenty minutes that passed seemed like hours. A nurse came into the room to clean up the area. She offered us water and showed us how to operate the TV controls, turning the TV on in the process.

Soon the doctor returned to explain their findings. Because they were uncertain if our baby had a heart problem or a collapsed lung, they needed to transport her to the local children's hospital for specialized care. The ambulance would be leaving with her immediately, and my husband needed to accompany her.

As the doctor exited the room, our attention was drawn to the television screen. The Believer's Voice of Victory broadcast was playing. As my husband turned up the volume of the TV, Kenneth Copeland was declaring Psalm 112:7, *"He shall not be afraid of evil tidings: his heart is fixed, trusting in the Lord."* We joined our hands, dealt with the fear of the moment, and placed our trust in God to help us.

The next time my husband was able to see our daughter was after they had admitted her into the children's hospital. She was in a clear, plastic oxygen tent with special lighting to treat jaundice. My husband laid his hands upon the tent and spoke healing words of life.

Within a few days, she was able to breathe more and more effectively, and the oxygen was incrementally turned down. My husband heard the doctor remark to a group of interns, "This is our miracle baby. She has healed herself." We knew God was the One responsible for the healing of our daughter.

Preparing for God's Plan

It would be years before I preached my first sermon, but the preparation phase began right away. I shared my testimony whenever the opportunity arose and served in the church in any and every capacity that was needed. My ministry began as I taught children in Sunday school and cleaned the church but continued over the years to include prison ministry, homeless outreach, and running various departments in the church. The Lord promoted my faithfulness with occasions to preach and teach as I grew in my relationship with the Word.

As the calling of God developed, Philip and I became pastors of a church in De Soto, Kansas, in December of 1998. The Lord instructed us to plant our second church in Little Rock, Arkansas, in 2015. At the time of this writing, we maintain the responsibilities in both locations, pastoring, teaching, and building faith.

Other churches have been established under our covering, and ministers birthed from our Bible college. God has entrusted us with a TV ministry that reaches across the country in English and Spanish. Philip and I have written numerous books to help people understand how to put the Word of God to work in their lives.

If you would have walked up to me as I stood on the street corner, jonesing for my next fix and waiting to turn the next trick, and said, "One day, God is going to put you on national TV. Your books will go around the world and help people meet Jesus Christ. You are going to preach the Gospel!" I would have laughed in your face. When the Bible says, *"But God hath chosen the foolish things of the world to confound the wise....*" (1 Corinthians 1:27), I think God was talking about me! It seems so foolish that God can take my mess and turn my life into something through which He can be glorified.

But what the Lord has done for me is "*...exceeding abundantly above all...*" I could have asked or thought (Ephesians 3:20). But here I am—and to God be the glory!

CHAPTER ELEVEN

POINTING TO JESUS

As the worship leader placed her fingers on the keys of the electric piano, the congregation lifted their hands to worship. I went forward to receive prayer along with others who responded to the minister's invitation to receive of God's anointing. There was no warning or indication to prepare me for what happened next. As the minister placed his hand on my head, my body crumpled to the floor. But I went somewhere else—somewhere in the realm of the spirit.

I looked around to see where I was and realized I was standing on a circular platform surrounded on every side by a huge crowd of people. This platform was lifted slightly above the ocean of people who were tightly sandwiched together, shoulder to shoulder. A sense of unrest—a desperate hopelessness—surged like an electric current through the multitude.

I was dressed in a dirty, torn outfit. To my surprise, I wasn't ashamed of the way I was dressed. Instead, I wanted everyone to see and understand why I was wearing the tattered garments. So, I lifted my voice to get the attention of the people. As I raised my voice, the desperate, hopeless faces turned their faces toward me to see my dirty clothes and hear what I had to say.

Their interest in my story seemed supernatural. As I described in detail what had happened to my outfit, the reason why my clothes had become so tattered and ragged, I could sense the shift in the atmosphere as the people began to process my words.

There was a moment in the telling of my story when I recognized I had the attention of the people. That moment was my purpose and aim. Every embarrassing detail, every uncomfortable explanation, they were shared to achieve this moment.

When I had their attention, I immediately pointed them to my Lord, Jesus Christ. He stood on a pedestal above us, brightly shining in His glory. As the people turned their faces to Him, they found hope. They encountered the One with the desire and ability to change their lives in the same way He had restored mine.

In my vision, I repeated this process over and over, gaining the attention of the crowds and quickly diverting their attention to Jesus. When the vision ended, I understood exactly what it meant. My assignment was clear. The tattered garments and shame of my past are instruments to draw people's attention to Jesus.

But the tattered garments by themselves would not inspire hope if people couldn't see the change in my life. The pedestal I stood on represents what the Lord has done to transform my life. He has filled my life with His goodness.

My Before and After Pictures

I love true stories, especially stories of transformation. My favorites are the extreme weight-loss testimonies because they show the before and after pictures that reveal how dramatically their lives are changed. In the same way, I want you to know the extreme turnaround the Lord has made in my life.

God's restoration in my life began the moment I received Jesus but has continued to work, making my life complete, stable, and full of His glory. If people only hear about the details of my life before God saved me, without receiving Jesus as Lord and allowing His Word to work in them, they will miss the restoration God wants to do in their lives.

In the second portion of this book, I will point you to Jesus and show you *how* the Word of God has rebuilt my life. I want you to know *how* God taught me who I am in Christ and *how* to recognize the voice and leading of His Spirit. Like a person who experienced a total-life makeover, I can say, "This is my life before Jesus became my Lord, and this is my life since I have been following Him."

Many people who hear my testimony are shocked when they see me. For instance, when people see my television program, they are shocked to find out that the woman preaching once sold her body or put a needle in her arm. They are shocked to discover that I attempted suicide, overdosed on drugs, and was arrested for attempted armed robbery.

The question that follows their amazement is: "*How* did it happen? *How* did your life change from one extreme to another?" A one-line answer like "Jesus Christ changed my life" isn't enough to help people see *how* God transformed my life.

In the following chapters, I want to point you to the specific truths that helped me grow spiritually and become established in who I am today. These fundamentals are still actively at work in my life, but they were added piece by piece as I grew in my relationship with the Lord.

When children learn to read, they begin by learning the letters of the alphabet and the sounds the letters make. These are fundamental pieces that a reader will always use. Even when they have advanced in their reading level, they are using these fundamentals without consciously realizing it. In our walk with God, He wants to establish us in the spiritual foundation that will provide a stable, steady growth.

But our spiritual foundations must be established securely. In reading, if someone advances to the next reading class without learning the basics of their previous class, they will struggle.

The same is true with our spiritual progress! I have met many believers who struggle with their past, their failures, and their flesh because they don't have a spiritual foundation. My friend, you don't have to fight that battle.

If these fundamentals are concepts you already know, read for the purpose of strengthening yourself in these truths. Don't skim or skip over them, thinking you don't need it. The repetition of truth establishes the revelation in your heart.

If you are a new believer who has just found freedom and these concepts are new to you, don't rush through this. Take the time to study and dig into God's Word with each of these truths. Let the Holy Spirit guide you in knowing how to apply God's Word to your situation.

If you are a family member or friend of someone caught in bondage to destruction, your faith can be productive for their freedom. In the same way that the Shunammite woman from 2 Kings 4:18-37 became a living instrument in the hand of God, you can be used by God to open the door of deliverance. I encourage you to read through the following chapters to identify your objective in prayer because you want the fundamentals that are outlined to be embraced and established in the lives of your loved ones. Your faith is involved in God's plan for your loved one and your authority in the realm of the spirit is vital.

This is not a sprint but a marathon. Pace yourself, and let's prepare for the finish line.

CHAPTER TWELVE

FUNDAMENTAL #1
MEET THE NEW YOU

When a person accepts Jesus as Lord, that person is made completely new. Being born again does not mean we are remodeled or refurbished. No! We are made new, and we are born of God!

Sadly, many believers don't realize what happened to them in the new birth, so they don't access the abilities that are available to them in Christ. They struggle and suffer through things they are equipped to overcome because they don't know Who lives in them. They continue to carry burdens of guilt and shame because they don't realize the blood cleared them and made them righteous.

Have you known someone who paid a hefty price for the newest, top-of-the-line smartphone but only used it to make phone calls? They might go so far as to learn how to take pictures with their phone, but they haven't uncovered the full potential of that expensive device. The same thing can be said about the new you in Christ. You have so much potential that you are unaware of until the Word of God reveals it to you. To find out what the "new you" can do, you need to read the Manufacturer's Handbook because you are completely new—with new features, abilities, and spiritual equipment. There is no other way to identify who you are, what you have, and what you can do without consulting the Bible, the book provided by the One who created you.

Who Am I?

Before Jesus saved me, I identified myself by my mistakes or the circumstances around me. If you had asked me, "Who are you?" I would have answered, "I am a junkie, a prostitute. I'm a miserable example of a mother."

The first thing the Lord taught me was that I could no longer identify with the mistakes I had made, the sins I had committed, or my arrest record on file at the county jail. I am not the same person—I am a new creature. The truth of this new identity is my reality.

Second Corinthians 5:17 is the first verse God established in my life to help me disconnect from my past.

> *Therefore if any person is [ingrafted] in Christ (the Messiah) he is a new creation (a new creature altogether); the old [previous moral and spiritual condition] has passed away. Behold, the fresh and new has come!* (2 Corinthians 5:17 AMPC)

Through this verse, the Lord showed me I was more than a remodeled, cleaned-up version of the old Michelle. The Greek word for *creature* describes a new creation that never existed before that moment of being born again. The "old Michelle" died with Christ, and the person I am today is born of God. I am a daughter of God who has never prostituted her body or stuck a needle in her arm!

Jesus said in John 3:7, *"...ye must be born again."* When I was born again, I became a new person. The person I was before I accepted Jesus as my Lord was involved in crime and drug addiction. But that is not who I am today. I am a woman who is pure, holy, and righteous in the presence of God.

It took some time and the renewing of my mind, but I allowed God's Word to identify me. In other words, I accepted what God said about me as truth even though I didn't feel different. When I didn't feel like I had changed, I verbally reminded myself, "I am not what I did. I am born of God. I am a new creature, and old things are passed away."

For me to try to live my new life in Christ while identifying myself as a drug addict, shoplifter, thief, or prostitute would have been impossible. I would have been a victim of mistaken identity, always presenting the old I.D. of the addicted, shame-filled woman. But God would have inspected my I.D. and said, "That is not you in that picture."

Feelings Are Unstable Identifiers

Are you consulting your feelings and emotions to locate your identity? If so, you may constantly change the perception of who you are. Unless your emotions and feelings are governed by God's Word and guided by your born-again spirit, they are not trustworthy.

If we base our identity purely on feelings, we will ask the wrong questions, such as: "Do I feel like God loves me? Do I feel accepted by God? Do I feel righteous?"

Well, what *exactly* does righteousness feel like? Are you expecting righteousness to produce goosebumps or some other type of noticeable feeling? You won't recognize righteousness with emotions or natural feelings.

For instance, I wake up every morning married, but I don't always *feel* married. What does "being married" *feel* like? I am married because of a covenant I entered with Philip Steele. We have a legal marriage document and a verbal commitment. It is a decision that Philip and I made. We are married, even on the days we don't *feel* like it.

In the same way, we become children of God when we receive Jesus Christ as our Savior and Lord. Regardless of how we feel, when we believe on Jesus, our faith connects us to the provision of salvation.

> *But as many as received him, to them gave he power to become the sons of God, even to them that believe on his name* (John 1:12).

Whether we feel like it or not, we are *legally* God's children. Sometimes we need to tell our feelings to get in line with God's Word. Act like the Bible is true and start living like a child of God. Begin to approach your Heavenly Father the way a child approaches their daddy—with eager, open arms.

We are in God's family—heirs of God and joint-heirs with Jesus Christ.

The Spirit Himself bears witness with our spirit that we are children of God, and if children, then heirs—heirs of God and joint heirs with Christ... (Romans 8:16-17 NKJV).

We may not feel worthy of an inheritance, but we are heirs because the Bible says so. If we wait for feelings to agree with what we read in the Word, we will miss most of what God has prepared for us. No matter what our feelings and emotions indicate, our identity is secure in Jesus, our Lord. But we must walk in the light of what the truth says about us to experience the benefits of it.

Allowing God's Word to establish our identity is the only accurate way to live our lives. We are born again by His Word, so we must let God's Word provide the foundation of our identity. We can give our attention to what our feelings say or accept what God says about who we are. God is always right, and His Word should hold greater influence than our feelings.

The Situation Cannot Properly Identify You

So, what evidence are you using to confirm your identity? Neither your past nor present circumstances can accurately identify who you are in Christ.

Are you looking at the past for details to describe who you are today? Searching your past might cause you to say, "I am a failure because I am divorced" or "I'm stupid because I quit school." The question to ask is this: Are your past mistakes an accurate and reliable indicator of who you really are? No!

Allowing a current situation to identify you isn't a good idea either. Suppose you are in a foreclosure on your house or out of work. In that case, you might identify yourself as a failure because of how the situation makes you feel.

You might look at the choices of your adult children and say, "I am a bad parent because my son is in prison." But that is not *who* you are!

Are you looking at how other people have treated you to confirm your identity? If so, you might say, "I am unlovable because my father left us." You might believe, "I am not a good woman because my husband had an affair." You might think, "There is something wrong with me because that person molested me when I was a child." The way other people treat us is not an accurate indicator of who we are.

Do You Have Your New I.D.?

The last time I renewed my driver's license, the woman processing my renewal asked me for my old license that was about to expire. She took the scissors from her desk and cut the corner off my driver's license, making it invalid. I wanted to stop her and explain, "Hey! I have kept up with that identification. I make sure I know where it is at all times. I carry it with me everywhere. I may need that old I.D."

Let me help you. You don't need your old I.D. anymore. You need to let God destroy the old ways of identifying yourself because they are invalid. You are not that same person! If you will get your kingdom identification and hold onto it, you will have access to the victory, wisdom, help, protection, and every other provision that belongs to you as a child of God.

Do you remember the first time you went to get your driver's license or another form of government identification? You had to show your birth certificate or social security card because you need evidence to prove who you are. God's Word provides the legal evidence we need to prove who we are and the position we hold in the kingdom of God.

Then, your driver's license includes your physical description, address, and birth date. With that I.D., you can open accounts, purchase a home, fly on an airplane, or apply for a position in a company. Without it, you will be hindered or restricted from many legal activities. Without our kingdom

I.D., our activities in the kingdom of God are limited or restricted. Kingdom benefits that legally belong to us as children of God, such as health, peace, and victory, require that we present the evidence of who we are.

Faith is how we connect to our identification. We believe with our hearts that Christ died as our sacrifice, our substitute, and that God raised Jesus from the dead. Our faith is spiritual substance, the evidence that we are raised from death to life.

> *For with the heart man believeth unto righteousness...* (Romans 10:10).

What we believe about the things Jesus accomplished by His death, burial, and resurrection will determine the access we have to the provisions that belong to us in the kingdom of God. For example, I believe Jesus was made to be sin for me. My faith in the fact that Jesus became sin for me connects me to the reality that I am made the righteousness of God in Him.

> *For he hath made him to be sin for us, who knew no sin; that we might be made the righteousness of God in him* (2 Corinthians 5:21).

If we don't believe we are born again as new creatures in Christ, we will continue to live like the sin-dominated people we were before salvation. Wrong thinking and wrong believing will produce wrong behavior. Instead, let's allow the light of God's Word to provide our perception!

For instance, if shame from my past tries to convince me that God won't hear my prayers, I need to identify myself, saying, "According to Romans 3:24, I am justified freely by God's grace through the redemption that is in Christ Jesus. In 1 John 5:14, the Bible assures me that God hears my prayers. This is the confidence I have in Him. If I ask anything according to His will, I know He hears me. And if I know He hears me, I know I have the thing I have asked of Him."

By believing in my heart and releasing that faith through my mouth, I am drawing my spiritual I.D. card out of my wallet and proving who I really am. My faith establishes my identity in that situation. When I resist the shame with the Word of God, the shame cannot override what my faith in Jesus Christ has established.

God provides us with legal documents to establish our new identity. You just need to know where to find them. So, here are some of the first steps to take:

Step #1 Get Your Death Certificate

God's scriptural documents testify to my death *with* Christ on the cross. Because I have this spiritual document in my possession (in my heart), it provides spiritually legal testimony that the old Michelle is dead.

If you don't have your death certificate, you have no proof that the "old you" is dead. It is your word against the overwhelming evidence of shame. It will be your testimony against the devil's accusations.

We don't want to try to argue our innocence without evidence. Remember, faith is the evidence, and faith comes by hearing the Word. We need to get our death certificates and keep them handy.

Where can we find the legal document to prove the old life of guilt is gone? We have a death certificate that is on record in heaven's legal archives! When Jesus died on the cross. He was crucified as our substitute. Because of Jesus' sacrifice and our faith in what He did, we have been crucified. Faith puts us on the cross with Jesus Christ. If we believe Jesus died *for* us, God credits it to our account.

In other words, when I acknowledged that Jesus was crucified *for* me, in my place, God deposited the value of Jesus' death on the cross into my account! Faith proves I died *with* Christ. So, here is my death certificate:

> *My old self has been crucified with Christ. It is no longer I who live, but Christ lives in me. So I live in this earthly body by trusting in the Son of God, who loved me and gave himself for me* (Galatians 2:20 NLT).

The old, guilt-ridden, and miserable Michelle died on the cross with Jesus Christ. Because I *know* I have been crucified with Christ, I learned not to buy into the lies that my feelings tried to tell me. I didn't let my past hold me in bondage to regret, beating myself up for all the mistakes I had made. I'm dead to that! Instead, I am so thankful that I am not who I used to be that it is hard to wipe the smile off my face!

Benefits of Having Your Death Certificate

If you have a death certificate, sin can't boss you around. We are not victims to sin. Sin cannot dominate us! If we don't yield to sin, we never *have* to sin because it doesn't hold a position of authority in our lives anymore.

When I was a drug addict, I obeyed the controlling, manipulating mandates of sin. Addiction dominated me, bossing me around. I obeyed what the addiction commanded me to do. But when I was crucified with Christ, God freed me from serving sin.

> *Knowing this, that our old man is crucified with him, that the body of sin might be destroyed, that henceforth we should not serve sin* (Romans 6:6).

Romans 6:6 in The Amplified Bible says, "*We know that our old (unrenewed) self was nailed to the cross with Him....*"

In God's Word Translation, it reads, "*We know that the person we used to be was crucified with him....*"

The old me has passed away, and I can testify, "I have been crucified, and my old self is dead. The penalty for my sin has been paid in full. I have a death certificate for the old me."

If sin puts pressure on me, I can resist it. I am under no obligation to serve sin. But this resistance begins by knowing that I am dead to sin.

> *Likewise you also, reckon yourselves to be dead indeed to sin, but alive to God in Christ Jesus our Lord. Therefore do not let sin reign in your mortal body, that you should obey it in its lusts. And do not present your members as instruments of unrighteousness to sin, but present yourselves to God as being alive from the dead, and your members as instruments of righteousness to God. For sin shall not have dominion over you, for you are not under law but under grace* (Romans 6:11-14 NKJV).

Did you see our instructions in these verses? First, we see, *"...reckon yourselves...."* That is an accounting term! It means we need to reconcile the account and look at the balance after all debits and credits are recorded. When we factor in the cross and Jesus' blood, our sin account will balance out at zero.

So, take account of the fact that you are *"...dead indeed to sin."* I love how this phrase is presented in The New Testament: An Expanded Translation by Kenneth Wuest. It reads, *"be constantly counting upon the fact that...you are those who have been separated from the sinful nature...."* We need to be so aware of the fact that we were crucified with Christ that we reconcile His victory over sin as our victory too!

Step #2 Find Where You Are Buried

If a death certificate has been issued to prove that we are dead, it seems appropriate that there should be a location *where* we are buried. The Bible provides proof that we were buried with Jesus Christ.

> *Therefore we were buried with Him through baptism into death, that just as Christ was raised from the dead by the glory of the Father, even so we also should walk in newness of life* (Romans 6:4 NKJV).

God's Word Translation says, *"When we were baptized into his death, we were placed into the tomb with him...."* If you were baptized, you have been buried in the tomb with Jesus. Now you have confirmation that the person you were before Christ is dead *and* buried.

Step #3 Get Your New Birth Certificate

This same verse says that we were raised from the dead *"...just as Christ was raised from the dead by the glory of the Father...."* When Jesus was raised from spiritual death, we were also raised from spiritual death and resurrected into His new life. Our faith in what God did through Jesus and what Jesus did for us is legal evidence to prove we are alive unto God.

Because we are dead to sin and alive in Christ, we can live differently. We can walk in the new life in Christ instead of the guilty, shame-filled life of the past.

We were buried therefore with Him by the baptism into death, so that just as Christ was raised from the dead by the glorious [power] of the Father, so we too might [habitually] live and behave in newness of life. For if we have become one with Him by sharing a death like His, we shall also be [one with Him in sharing] His resurrection [by a new life lived for God] (Romans 6:4-5 AMPC).

Notice the phrase found in verse 4, *"so we too might [habitually] live and behave in newness of life."* God raised us from the deadness of our sinful past so that we can habitually live and behave as the new person we are in Christ.

Step #4 Update the Address on Your I.D.

If you move, you have to take proof of your new residence and update your identification card. As you are establishing your new I.D. card in the kingdom of God, don't put your old address. Make sure you present Ephesians 2:6 to prove your new position.

And raised us up together, and made us sit together in the heavenly places in Christ Jesus (Ephesians 2:6 NKJV).

These documents prove you are crucified, buried, resurrected, and seated together in Christ Jesus. Get your spiritual birth certificate out and meditate on who you are now—in Christ. Establish God's Word as your reality, and let your true identity guide your attitude, actions, and decisions.

You aren't a product of what happened to you. You aren't what other people have said about you, and you aren't what you did or didn't do. You are who God says you are, crucified with Christ, buried into His death, resurrected into His new life, and seated together with Him in authority.

Taking Action

1. Make a list of the Scriptures that help you clarify your identity in Christ. Read them out loud daily and make them personal. For example, "Romans 6 says that the old me is crucified with Christ. From now on, I don't serve sin. I am a new creature in Christ Jesus, and I am born of God (Romans 6:6, 2 Corinthians 5:17).

2. Ask the Lord to help you identify specific areas in the way you view yourself that are in conflict with who you are in Christ. For instance, if you think you are a failure or that you will never amount to anything, look for the Scriptures that call you victorious.

   a. We are more than conquerors (Romans 8:37).

   b. God gives us the victory through our Lord Jesus Christ (1 Corinthians 15:57).

   c. God always causes us to triumph in Christ (2 Corinthians 2:14).

My Declaration

Today—and every day—I am determined to see myself as God created me in Christ Jesus. I submit my mind, will, and emotions to the authority of God's Word, and I resist the attack of the enemy's thoughts to confuse me. I am righteous because Jesus became sin for me so that I would be made the righteousness of God in Him (2 Corinthians 5:21). *I am a child of God, and I have a full inheritance with Jesus Christ* (John 1:12, Romans 8:14-17, Galatians 3:26). *God has given me wisdom, revelation, and strength in my innermost being* (Ephesians 1:17-18). *I choose to see myself with the new identity Christ Jesus has provided for me.*

Praying for Someone You Love

One of the most valuable things you can provide for your loved one is a prayer supply. By using your faith and applying what you know about the will of God for them, you can make tremendous power available that is dynamic in its working (James 5:16 AMPC). Here are some vital points you can pray for them to receive:

Father, in the name of Jesus, I approach Your throne to receive help for my loved one. I ask for the light of the Gospel of Jesus Christ to shine

*brightly in the eyes of their understanding, caus-
ing them to clearly see Your love and the plan You
have for their lives. As they accept Jesus Christ as
their Lord and Savior, I ask You to lead them
through Your Word to see themselves as new creatures in Christ—free from the sin of their past
and alive with Your very life. As Your represen-
tative, I exercise dominion over Satan, the god of
this world, and break the control of deception and
the lies that have worked to hold my loved one in
bondage. I thank You, Father, that the path of my
loved one is as the shining light and will continue
to grow brighter and brighter* (Proverbs 4:18).

Chapter Thirteen

Fundamental #2
Learn to Hear
God in His Word

The first time I heard someone say, "The Lord spoke to me," I thought they were strange. My first thought was, *Really? You "heard" from God? I don't think so!* But it was a phrase that I continued to hear in regular conversation with the people who attended our church.

They would say things like "I was praying, and the Lord said to me..." or "The Lord spoke to my heart...." Once I got over the shock, I became curious, and I wanted to know how to hear from Him too. If anybody needed to hear from God, it was me!

So, I asked the people in the church. If I thought they had any spiritual know-how, I brought it up in conversation. "How do you hear from God?" Sadly, very few people offered any advice. Most people told me to "just listen."

One of the few people who did offer a response said, "After you pray, sit quietly and let God talk." I prayed my prayers the next morning and then sat silently, waiting to hear

God speak. I tried to listen with my ears and heard nothing. I tried this for a few days without any success.

Recognizing the Voice of God through His Word

But I didn't give up. Instead, I continued asking different people how to hear God's voice. Finally, I asked my pastor's wife, who really helped me. She said, "Michelle, if you will learn to recognize God's voice by reading what He has already spoken in His Word, you will recognize Him when He speaks to your spirit." She explained that the voice of the Spirit of God would NEVER contradict the written Word. She encouraged me to let the Word of God be my foundation. By doing this, I would make it easier for the Spirit of God to lead me.

So, instead of sitting quietly in a room, waiting for God's voice to ring in my eardrums, I began to put His words in my heart. To my surprise, God's Word began to speak to me! I encountered answers as I was reading. God comforted me with Scriptures and brought light to situations as I saw His instructions.

The first time God spoke to me through His Word is still so vividly clear to me. I had not been saved very long, and the situations surrounding my life were a hot mess! One of the family members who was infuriated that I was trying to get custody of my children had threatened to shoot me. They owned a gun and knew how to shoot it, so I was dealing with the fear produced by their threat.

Then, someone broke into their house and stole the urn that held Bo's remains, and they accused me of doing it. I tried to convince them that I was innocent. I had been in church all evening, for crying out loud! But they wouldn't believe me and began to say, "We are coming over right now. If you don't give us the urn, we are going to kill you."

I was still living with the friends who had witnessed to me and brought me to church. They weren't as concerned about the threats. They prayed with me and went to bed for the night, leaving me in the living room alone with fear.

I spread my sheet and blanket out on the couch and fluffed my pillow, trying to stop my mind from thinking about the venom in their voices. With each passing car, my heart was racing as I listened to hear if it would turn into the driveway. Thoughts bombarded my mind saying, *"How am I going to sleep? What am I going to do if they come here demanding something I don't have?"*

Finally, I decided to open my Bible. As it fell open on my lap, the letters stood off the page as if under a magnifying glass, *"I, even I, am he that comforteth you: who art thou, that thou shouldest be afraid of a man that shall die, and of the son of man which shall be made as grass"* (Isaiah 51:12). The words melted away the fear and torment that had been so prevalent moments before. The presence of God was so near to me at that moment as His Word strengthened me. I don't think the audible voice of God would have given me any more courage or comfort than I received that night through His Word.

Since that evening, I have encountered many other occasions when the Lord has ministered to me through His Word. While I have never plopped open my Bible and had a Scripture stand up on the page like it did that night, God has taught me how to know His voice as I read or study His Word.

Later, when the Lord needed to speak specific things to my heart, I recognized it was the same voice Who had spoken to me through the Bible. I could trust and respond with confidence because I had already been following Him.

The Word Provides Our Stability

And wisdom and knowledge shall be the stability of thy times, and strength of salvation: the fear of the LORD is his treasure (Isaiah 33:6).

From the beginning of my walk with God, He taught me to see His Word in a way I had never thought of it before I was saved. I knew the Bible was a "different" book, a book my grandma read. But I had never considered it to be something *I* needed to read.

Even though I was a good reader, I was intimidated by the King James version, using words like *thou, thee, doest,* and *saith*. In addition, I wasn't sure *where* to start reading. Do I start at the beginning? Do I start with the New Testament? It can be frustrating to someone new to the things of God to tell them they need to read their Bible every day. But God helped me by showing me how valuable His Word is to the stability of my life.

While I was very thankful to be free from the drugs, I was even more grateful to be free from the guilt and shame. The destruction that was once the driving force of my life was gone, and I had a peace I had never known. I didn't want to lose that peace!

God revealed something to me in His Word that made me realize I need to stay full of the Word, which protects me from the enemy gaining an entrance back into my life. In the following text, Jesus is teaching us how the adversary operates.

> *No sooner however has the foul spirit gone out of the man, then he roams about in places where there is no water, seeking rest but finding none Then he says, "I will return to my house that I left;" and he comes and finds it unoccupied, swept clean, and in good order. Then he goes and brings back with him seven other spirits more wicked than himself, and they come in and dwell there; and in the end that man's condition becomes worse than it was at first* (Matthew 12:43-45 WNT).

Jesus taught us the attack methods of the enemy so we can be on guard against a counterattack. The Lord explains that the enemy will return, looking to see if there is any room for him to get back into that person's life. In verse 44, it uses the word *unoccupied*. The Bible in Basic English says, *"...he sees that there is no one in it...."*

When I understood this, I determined I didn't want the devil to look at me and find me empty! I wanted to know, "How can I stay full of God?" I discovered that I needed to develop a relationship with God's Word. The Bible is not just a book about God. The Word is God! The Bible is God speaking to us. The Word of God is alive! Before Jesus had a body, He existed as the Word of God.

> *In the beginning was the Word, and the Word was with God, and the Word was God* (John 1:1).
>
> *And the Word was made flesh, and dwelt among us, (and we beheld his glory, the glory as of the only begotten of the Father,) full of grace and truth* (John 1:14).

We can know God through His Word and grow in our relationship with Him by interacting with His Word. God established His Word as the method to reveal and transmit His will into our lives.

God's Word Is Spirit and Life

The supernatural ability and life of God is contained in the Word of God. God placed His life in His Word so He could distribute that life to us.

In him was life; and the life was the light of men
(John 1:4).

While the Bible includes God's plans, His love for us, and His will, God's Word is alive. According to Hebrews 4:12 (NKJV), *"...the word of God is living and powerful...."*

We should guard against reading the Word of God in the same way we scroll through social media or scan the page of a newspaper. God's Word deserves a holy approach. We should open our Bibles with the thought in our mind, *This is God speaking to me.*

God's Word is not alive with the temporary kind of life like an animal or a plant but with eternal life. The word *eternal* describes something that is never diminishing in power and never diminishing in value. *The Vine's Expository Dictionary of New Testament Words* uses the following phrase to describe *eternal:* "persons and things which are in their nature endless." For example, the blood of Jesus is eternal because it will never diminish in value.

God uses His words to transmit His eternal life to us, so we can live a "never diminishing in power, never diminishing in value" kind of life by His Word.

It is the Spirit who gives life; the flesh profits nothing. The words that I speak to you are spirit, and they are life (John 6:63 NKJV).

The power of God that resides in His words is the key to our success in life. When Jesus quoted Deuteronomy 8:3, saying, *"Man shall not live by bread alone, but by every word that proceeds from the mouth of God,"* He was identifying our spiritual nutrition. We need the Word of God more than we need natural food! The Word of God contains what we need to fulfill the plan of God.

When instructing Joshua, the Lord advised him to keep the Word in His mouth. The Old Testament word *meditate* includes the meaning "to mutter."

> *This Book of the Law shall not depart from your mouth, but you shall meditate in it day and night, that you may observe to do according to all that is written in it. For then you will make your way prosperous, and then you will have good success* (Joshua 1:8 NKJV).

If you have the Word in your mouth, you have possession of it. You are spiritually "holding" that promise as you mutter it to yourself. Proverbs 18:21 says that death and life are in the power of the tongue. The word *power* is also defined as *hand*.

Your born-again spirit has a hand! With that spiritual hand of the tongue, you can hold spiritual things. You may not be able to grasp peace with your physical hand, but you can place Isaiah 26:3 (NKJV) in your mouth and hold it with your spiritual hand, saying, "You will keep me in perfect peace because my mind stays on You, and I trust in You."

Did you notice the Lord told Joshua, *"...you will make your way prosperous..."?* Joshua's outcome was not entirely up to God; it depended on what Joshua did with God's Word.

What happens in *our* lives is not entirely up to God either. We can choose to meditate in His Word—day and night—until we have the inner image of His plan imprinted in our hearts. Then, we will walk in His success.

> *Blessed is the man who walks not in the counsel of the ungodly, nor stands in the path of sinners, nor sits in the seat of the scornful; But his delight is in the law of the LORD, and in His law he meditates day and night. He shall be like a tree planted by the rivers of water, that brings forth its fruit in its season, whose leaf also shall not wither; and whatever he does shall prosper* (Psalm 1:1-3 NKJV).

Again, the Scriptures point to the Word laying the groundwork for our productivity, longevity, and success. So, if you want to thrive, here is the key! God's Word is spirit and life!

We can find God's will for every detail and decision of our lives by His Word. The more we understand God and His ways, the more accurately we align with His plan.

That has happened to me! Every day, I walk in more of God's Word than I saw or understood the day before. The Lord is leading me and teaching me, line upon line, precept upon precept, here a little, there a little. As a result, my life grows stronger, and things keep improving.

If Jesus Is Lord, His Word Governs

Since Jesus is my Lord, His Word should have the authority to govern my actions, thoughts, and decisions. If His Word doesn't have authority in my life, am I really submitted to Jesus? The Lord asked in Luke 6:46, *"And why call ye me, Lord, Lord, and do not the things which I say?"* Maybe you have heard the saying, "The proof of the pudding is in the eating." In other words, we prove the position Jesus has in our lives by how we obey His instructions.

For instance, Jesus said, *"And whenever you stand praying, if you have anything against anyone, forgive him and let it drop (leave it, let it go), in order that your Father Who is in heaven may also forgive you your [own] failings and shortcomings and let them drop"* (Mark 11:25 AMPC). If I hold onto a grudge and refuse to forgive someone, I am not submitting to Jesus. He said, *"...if you have anything against anyone...."* No matter how badly someone has hurt me, I want to submit to Jesus more than hold onto the unforgiveness.

In another teaching, Jesus told us not to worry. Does the Word govern us where worry is concerned? Do I have the "right" to worry?

Therefore do not worry and be anxious, saying, What are we going to have to eat? or, What are we going to have to drink? or, What are we going to have to wear? For the Gentiles (heathen) wish for and crave and diligently seek all these things, and your heavenly Father knows well that you need them all. But seek (aim at and strive after) first of all His kingdom and His righteousness (His way of doing and being right), and then all these things taken together will be given you besides So do not worry or be anxious about tomorrow, for tomorrow will have worries and anxieties of its own. Sufficient for each day is its own trouble (Matthew 6:31-34 AMPC).

In Philippians 4:6 (AMPC), the Word of God says, *"Do not fret or have any anxiety about anything...."* That instruction is not optional. We can't choose to obey the easy parts and neglect the commands that put pressure on us to change. No! If Jesus is Lord, His Word governs us.

Created Things Will Respond to the Word

Everything that exists in this universe was created by Jesus—the Word of God.

All things were made by him; and without him was not any thing made that was made (John 1:3).

*For by him were all things created, that are in
heaven, and that are in earth, visible and invisible,
whether they be thrones, or dominions, or princi-
palities, or powers: all things were created by him,
and for him: And he is before all things, and by
him all things consist* (Colossians 1:16-17).

Because the Word is the origin or substance of created
things, these things will respond to the Word when we apply
it correctly. God shows us how this works in Isaiah 55:11.

*So shall My word be that goes forth out of My
mouth: it shall not return to Me void [without
producing any effect, useless], but it shall accomplish that which I please and purpose, and it shall
prosper in the thing for which I sent it* (Isaiah
55:11 AMPC).

While this is an example of how God uses His Word to
change a situation, He wants us to become skilled in applying His Word in the same manner. Time after time, Jesus
demonstrated it for us by speaking to natural things, and
they obeyed Him. In Mark 4, we find that the wind and sea
obeyed Jesus when He spoke.

*And he arose, and rebuked the wind, and said unto
the sea, Peace, be still. And the wind ceased, and
there was a great calm. And he said unto them,
Why are ye so fearful? How is it that ye have no*

faith? And they feared exceedingly, and said one to another, What manner of man is this, that even the wind and the sea obey him? (Mark 4:39-41)

Jesus *rebuked* and *said*. He spoke to things, and the things obeyed Him. In another instance, we see that Jesus even spoke to a fever, and the fever obeyed Him.

And he arose out of the synagogue, and entered into Simon's house. And Simon's wife's mother was taken with a great fever; and they besought him for her. And he stood over her, and rebuked the fever; and it left her: and immediately she arose and ministered unto them (Luke 4:38-39).

Too many believers leave this use of words for God and Jesus. But the Lord intends for us to operate this way too. He said in Matthew 17:20 (NKJV), *"...if you have faith as a mustard seed, you will say to this mountain, 'Move from here to there,' and it will move; and nothing will be impossible for you."* If we will speak His Word, we can operate His faith and receive His results!

The Integrity of the Word

For ever, O LORD, thy word is settled in heaven (Psalm 119:89).

The word *settled* means "to stand, stand upright, be set (over), establish."[1] God's Word is the most stable thing you will ever encounter in this life. The winds of adversity can't move God's Word. The struggles and storms of life won't break the Word.

Jesus reveals that His words are more sure, more reliable than the sky above our heads and the earth beneath our feet.

> *Heaven and earth shall pass away, but my words shall not pass away* (Matthew 24:35).

This is the building material God has given us to establish our lives. We are designed to frame, fashion, arrange, and put our lives in order by the Word of God (Hebrews 11:3). The Word won't change, weaken, or fall apart.

If you want to test two types of metal to find out which metal is more durable, you will perform an integrity test. For instance, the integrity of copper is weaker than the integrity of steel or iron.

The Word of God is the most durable material available. In every test of integrity, God's Word will prevail. That is why you want your life built on the Word of God. Jesus said it this way:

> *Whosoever cometh to me, and heareth my sayings, and doeth them, I will shew you to whom he is like: He is like a man which built an house, and digged deep, and laid the foundation on a rock: and when the flood arose, the stream beat vehemently upon that house, and could not shake it: for it was founded upon a rock* (Luke 6:47-48).

When we make the effort to build our lives, health, finances, marriages, and other relationships on the Word of

God, we have a stability that cannot be found anywhere else. Storms are going to come to everybody, but stability in the storm is for those who have their lives built on the Word.

Abiding Will Access an Abundance

Jesus said we need to *abide* in Him, and His words need to *abide* in us. As you read this passage, notice how many times the Lord emphasized that word *abide*.

> *Abide in Me, and I in you. As the branch cannot bear fruit of itself, unless it abides in the vine, neither can you, unless you abide in Me. "I am the vine, you are the branches. He who abides in Me, and I in him, bears much fruit; for without Me you can do nothing. If anyone does not abide in Me, he is cast out as a branch and is withered; and they gather them and throw them into the fire, and they are burned. If you abide in Me, and My words abide in you, you will ask what you desire, and it shall be done for you. By this My Father is glorified, that you bear much fruit; so you will be My disciples* (John 15:4-8 NKJV.)

How does Jesus abide in us? He abides in us to the measure that His words abide in us. He said in verse four, *"Abide in Me and I in you...."* But in verse seven, Jesus identifies how He abides in us when He says, *"If you abide in Me and*

My words abide in you...." How do we help the Word abide in us?

Have you ever been reading the Bible and thinking to yourself, *What did I just read?* Well, I have. There have been times I found it hard to concentrate or comprehend what I was reading. I had to learn how to give attention to God's Word.

> *My son, give attention to my words; Incline your ear to my sayings. Do not let them depart from your eyes; Keep them in the midst of your heart; For they are life to those who find them, and health to all their flesh* (Proverbs 4:20-22 NKJV).

Getting the Word of God into our hearts is the objective. When we continually hear and read God's Word, we are depositing the light and life of that Word into our born-again spirits. His words are life and health to us as they enter and flow from our hearts. If the Word is not deposited in the heart, it can't release the life and light it contains.

If you deposit a paycheck in your bank account, you can make debits based on the deposit. When your account begins to get low, you need another deposit. If you continue making spiritual debits without spiritual deposits, you will get yourself in spiritual trouble.

Years ago, my husband and I decided that we hated living paycheck to paycheck. Instead of making a deposit and spending down to nothing before the next paycheck, we set a budget. We kept a close eye on our extra spending and kept a certain amount in the account. We must do the same thing with our Word supply. If we maintain daily deposits, we won't be overdrawn in our spiritual supply!

We want a fullness of the Word like Jesus spoke of in Matthew 12:34 (NKJV), when He said, *"...for out of the abundance of the heart the mouth speaks."* This verse shows us how we will know when the heart is full. The mouth will speak!

Taking Action

1. Develop the discipline to spend time in the Word of God every day. Proverbs 4:20-22 says that the Word needs to be in our eyes, in our ears, and in our hearts. Add Joshua 1:8 to the list to include putting the Word in your mouth.

   a. Load preaching podcasts on your phone or tablet. If your church has a YouTube or Roku channel, subscribe to it. When you are driving, listen to the preaching of the Word. Instead of bingeing on TV shows, put God's Word in your heart. Take notes or make an outline of the teaching so you can study it again.

   b. Instead of trying to read multiple chapters, give attention to specific things the

Lord is prompting you to learn. For instance, if you need to know more about righteousness, look for teachings or verses on the subject of righteousness.

2. Make the commitment to the Lord to be a doer of the Word. Let the Word of God direct and correct you. For example, when Malachi 3:10 speaks to you about bringing your tithe, the first tenth of your income, don't look for reasons why you shouldn't do it (i.e., tithing isn't valid, I need my money more than God needs my money, it's Old Testament, etc.). All of that mental reasoning will hinder you from the blessing of being a doer of God's Word.

My Declaration

I commit to give my attention and focus to the Word of God and to feed my born-again spirit on God's Word continually. I consider the words of God's mouth to be more necessary for me than food (Job 23:12). *The Word of God is life to me, and I will hide God's Word in my heart so that I won't sin against Him* (Proverbs 4:22, Psalm 119:11). *As I hear God's words and receive His sayings, I will walk in right paths, my steps will not be hindered, and I will not stumble* (Proverbs 4:10-12). *I commit to be a doer of the Word of God!*

Praying for Someone You Love

As I pray for the spiritual strength of my loved one, I come to You in Jesus' name. I specifically ask that You strengthen, complete, and perfect them, making them what they ought to be, equipping them with everything good that they may carry out Your will. I thank You that You are working in the life of my loved one to accomplish what is pleasing in Your sight (Hebrews 13:21). *Lord, help my loved one to learn how to trust in Your Word as a source of light for their decisions and as the spiritual nutrition to help them grow in Christ. Send people across their paths to confirm the Word You have already spoken to them. I ask You to grant them boldness to act on the Word of God as it is revealed to them.*

Note

1. Strong, James. "H5324 nāṣab." *The New Strong's Expanded Exhaustive Concordance of the Bible.* Red letter ed. Thomas Nelson, 2010.

CHAPTER FOURTEEN

FUNDAMENTAL #3 APPLY THE BLOOD CORRECTLY

The first time I heard a sermon about the blood of Jesus, I thought to myself, *Why are we talking about blood in church?* It took a little while for me to warm up to the idea of the preacher talking about blood, animal sacrifices, and Abraham taking Isaac to an altar. I am so glad I didn't follow the impulse to leave that service.

What I have learned about the blood of Jesus has provided me with supernatural freedom from guilt and shame. Because of my faith in the blood of Jesus, I have confidence in dealing with God and courage when I deal with the enemy.

At the end of my testimony, I shared with you two experiences that happened after I was saved. After Philip and I married, we were expecting our first child, which we lost in a miscarriage. Philip wanted to believe that God would help us, but shame hindered my faith.

The thought came into my mind that this was happening because of the abortion that had occurred years before. Even though I knew Jesus had forgiven me, clearing me of the guilt of the abortion, I was still ashamed.

The second experience happened a few years later. I had grown in the Word and had a different response to a similar situation. When our next child was born, she experienced trauma in the birth canal that caused her lung to collapse. At the time, we didn't know what had happened. We just witnessed her skin turning blue as she struggled to breathe. Then, the nurses took her out of the room, eventually sending her to the local children's hospital, where she stayed in ICU for over a week.

But the blood of Jesus is what made a difference in the victory we experienced in the second situation. In one situation, I yielded to shame, but in the other, I stood in faith. I want to share with you what I learned because it is a vital part of my progress.

The blood of Jesus is not supposed to only be used one time when we are born again. Instead, Jesus' blood should be a constant part of our spiritual activity.

There is a difference between guilt and shame, and the blood of Jesus is the weapon we use against them both. This truth helped me break free from the shame I was still carrying from my past—the shame that caused me to draw back from God's help.

The Difference Between Guilt and Shame

Guilt comes from an offense or violation, the result of whatever you did that was wrong. Guilt is the standing in which your action or transgression has placed you. A person can be *found* guilty of committing a violation or crime. And if, for example, you confess to something wrong you have done, you would say, "I *am* guilty." In so doing, you would be describing the state in which your transgression has placed you.

But shame is the feeling or emotional pain in your conscience that is caused by your guilt or the guilt of someone else who violates you. You can feel and experience shame. But shame isn't just felt in your emotions. Your subconscious mind also experiences a sense of shame. It is a painful feeling that reaches into your thoughts, perceptions and can even be attached to your memories.

Both guilt and shame hinder our approach to God but in two different ways. Specifically, guilt affects the way God can relate to us, while shame affects the way we relate to God.

When I first gave my life to Jesus Christ, I successfully put faith in the blood of Jesus that I was free of the guilty verdict. I believed Jesus paid the price for the sins I had committed and that they were not laid to my charge.

But I stopped at that first application of the blood of Jesus and never released faith in His blood to purge my conscience. That is why shame was still actively working in my life. God could reach me, but I was having trouble connecting with God.

Shame stayed hidden in my subconscious mind. So, whenever I felt or experienced shame, I would ask myself, *What did I do? Where did I sin?* I went to the altar to repent a lot in those days. I was repenting for the way I felt, trying to remove the shameful feeling with the same method I had used to remove guilt.

We have a great example of the two different applications of the blood in the Bible illustrated in the sacrifices and ceremonies of the Old Testament. Under the Old Covenant, there was a difference in the way people dealt with their guilt compared to the way they dealt with being unclean, the shameful condition caused by their guilt. They had to offer a sacrifice for their guilt. But there was a different method used to deal with their unclean condition—the shame.

The Penalty Paid

First, let's see how Jesus dealt with our guilt. Guilt requires judgment. Because God is just, He cannot pretend the act that caused our guilt never happened.

The penalty for the guilt caused by sin is death. None of us stood a chance because we were all guilty of sin. That's why Jesus left His position in heaven and willingly came to the earth as a man. He was the only One qualified to die and pay this price.

God created the first man and placed him in the Garden of Eden with the instruction to *"Be fruitful and multiply..."* (Genesis 1:22). Every person born in Adam's lineage would have his fundamental characteristics.

But before Adam reproduced, he sinned. Sin would now be passed on to every person born through his bloodline.

Each man, woman, and child was born into the sin-lineage of Adam. We all deserved to die and owed our lives in payment for our sins.

God then sent Jesus as a man. The Bible calls Jesus "the last Adam."

> *Thus it is written, The first man Adam became a living being (an individual personality); the last Adam (Christ) became a life-giving Spirit [restoring the dead to life]* (1 Corinthians 15:45 AMPC).

When we receive Jesus as Lord of our lives, we are reborn according to the pattern of Jesus and with His characteristics. We now have His attributes of righteousness and holiness. We come off the "spiritual assembly line" with the same qualities as Jesus Christ. We were sinners like the first Adam, but we are now righteous like the last Adam.

> *And just as we have borne the image [of the man] of dust, so shall we and so let us also bear the image [of the Man] of heaven* (1 Corinthians 15:49 AMPC).

To provide the spiritual connection for our rebirth, Jesus, the last Adam, had to undo what the first Adam did. Jesus had to regain what Adam lost by dealing with the guilt Adam caused and passed on to us.

Remember, guilt requires judgment, and Jesus had to die to pay the penalty. No other person could die and accomplish what the death of God's sinless Son accomplished. Jesus tasted death for every person. He did this to provide us with the opportunity to receive the life and nature of God.

In the Old Testament, the death of the animal on the altar substituted for the death of the person. But this substitution only lasted a year. The people had to return the following year with another animal and go through the same process of substitution again.

Also, the people were only covering their sin because the blood of an animal wasn't valuable enough to pay for their sin to be completely cleansed once and for all.

The old system under the law of Moses was only a shadow, a dim preview of the good things to come, not the good things themselves. The sacrifices under that system were repeated again and again, year after year, but they were never able to provide perfect cleansing for those who came to worship (Hebrews 10:1 NLT).

Because the people could never completely cleanse the sin, they were never able to relate to God in the way He wanted. The guilt was always standing in their way, and the shame was embedded deep down in their conscience. They perceived themselves as unacceptable and unclean.

If they could have provided perfect cleansing, the sacrifices would have stopped, for the worshipers

would have been purified once for all time, and
their feelings of guilt would have disappeared
(Hebrews 10:2 NLT).

God's perfect Son knew this and willingly offered to
change the situation. Jesus knew His Heavenly Father wanted
to have a strong, personal relationship with every person.
God wanted the liberty to love us as His own children. He
wanted every person to have the liberty to enjoy and partic-
ipate in this relationship without any presence of guilt or a
sense of shame.

In Chapter 10 of Hebrews, we see the conversation Jesus
had with the Father:

> *That is why, when Christ came into the world, he*
> *said to God, "You did not want animal sacrifices or*
> *sin offerings. But you have given me a body to offer.*
> *You were not pleased with burnt offerings or other*
> *offerings for sin. Then I said, 'Look, I have come to*
> *do your will, O God—as is written about me in the*
> *Scriptures'"* (Hebrews 10:5-7 NLT).

God loved us so much that He was willing to offer His
only Son to bring us into His kingdom and make us His children. When God gave Jesus, He sacrificed His all. Jesus was
His only son. But through Jesus Christ, God would be able to
have many descendants. Look at this explanation in the Book
of Isaiah:

But it was the LORD's good plan to crush him and cause him grief. Yet when his life is made an offering for sin, he will have many descendants. He will enjoy a long life, and the LORD's good plan will prosper in his hands. When he sees all that is accomplished by his anguish, he will be satisfied. And because of his experience, my righteous servant will make it possible for many to be counted righteous, for he will bear all their sins. I will give him the honors of a victorious soldier, because he exposed himself to death. He was counted among the rebels. He bore the sins of many and interceded for rebels (Isaiah 53:10-12 NLT).

Jesus interceded for rebels, and I was one of those rebels! He received the punishment for my guilt so that I could receive His right standing with God. So, it pleases God when we live our lives without guilt because Jesus died to purchase that freedom for us.

The Blood Is Our Approach to God

What God really wanted was to have a close, loving relationship with us. This has only been available since the blood of Jesus was poured out on the cross. Before that, the ability to approach God was limited.

Let's look at the way the Old Testament worshippers had to approach God. In seeing their limited access, we can realize and appreciate how much better our relationship is because of the blood of Jesus.

The first reference to blood in the Bible is implied. When Adam and Eve sinned in the Garden of Eden, the glory that once covered them departed. They hid from God because they realized they were naked (Genesis 3:8-10). God used the skins of animals to cover Adam and Eve (Genesis 3:21).

This meant that God had to shed the blood of animals to cover the guilt of the first man and woman. So, even though they had disobeyed God and caused the separation in their relationship with God, God, out of love, still cared for them by providing them with this covering.

The next implication of blood is seen when Adam and Eve's sons brought offerings to the Lord.

> *When it was time for the harvest, Cain presented some of his crops as a gift to the LORD Abel also brought a gift—the best of the firstborn lambs from his flock. The LORD accepted Abel and his gift, but he did not accept Cain and his gift. This made Cain very angry, and he looked dejected. "Why are you so angry?" the LORD asked Cain. "Why do you look so dejected? You will be accepted if you do what is right. But if you refuse to do what is right, then watch out! Sin is crouching at the door, eager to control you. But you must subdue it and be its master"* (Genesis 4:3-7 NLT).

God talked to Cain, instructing Cain on how to approach Him. God wanted to accept Cain's offering, but Cain failed to approach God under the covering of blood. Cain wanted to approach God through his efforts. The problem was that Cain's efforts could not wash away the guilt of sin, and all of Cain's hard work could not cleanse the shame.

God told Cain and Abel the acceptable way to approach Him. In Hebrews 11:4, we see that Abel was moved by faith when he brought his sacrifice to God.

> *It was by faith that Abel brought a more acceptable offering to God than Cain did. Abel's offering gave evidence that he was a righteous man, and God showed his approval of his gifts. Although Abel is long dead, he still speaks to us by his example of faith* (Hebrews 11:4 NLT).

God wasn't playing favorites when He accepted Abel's offering and refused Cain's. Instead, Abel approached God with the blood of his lambs, as God had instructed him to do.

God was operating within the limits that mankind's guilt had placed on the relationship between God and man. Because God is holy and mankind had fallen into sin, God could not have the interaction with people that He really wanted.

In our society, when a person is placed in prison, they have restrictions on the extent to which they can interact with their family. Prisoners have limited time and contact with the people they love. Before Jesus shed His blood, the Heavenly Father must have felt like He was visiting His children in prison. Guilt held God at a distance from the people He had created for fellowship.

God truly loved Cain and encouraged Cain to properly approach Him by bringing the blood of an animal, as Abel had done. God told Cain that he would be accepted if he did the right thing. In this way, God gave Cain the method to cover his guilt.

A Lesson of Substitution

> *For the life of the body is in its blood. I have given you the blood on the altar to purify you, making you right with the LORD. It is the blood, given in exchange for a life, that makes purification possible* (Leviticus 17:11 NLT).

> *...because blood contains life. I have given this blood to you to make peace with me on the altar. Blood is needed to make peace with me* (Leviticus 17:11 GW).

God had to teach His people the reason for the blood. He explained that the life is in the blood. Your blood is the force of your life because it carries life to every part of your body. If your blood was poured out of your body, your life would flow out with it.

The blood of the innocent lamb on the altar represented the life of that innocent lamb. God said, *"...I have given you the blood on the altar to purify you..."* (Leviticus 17:11, NLT).

The blood of Jesus makes peace with God. But in the Old Testament, the animal blood was a temporary solution. Nonetheless, animal blood on earthly altars kept mankind connected to God until Jesus, the Lamb of God, could pour out His blood on the cross, carry it to the heavenly altar, and secure our permanent approach to Father God.

When the worshippers in the Old Testament brought their lambs as a sacrificial offering to God, they did so with the understanding that their lambs took their place. Generally, it was a lamb raised in their flock. They spent time with this lamb. So, to sacrifice the little lamb on the altar was a serious moment.

They would observe the priest as he cut the throat of the innocent lamb to allow the lamb's blood to flow out onto the altar. They could say, "The lamb is dying in my place. It is the death I deserve to receive. I am purified by the life of the lamb." The lamb's innocence was exchanged for their guilt. Every sacrifice was supposed to invoke this thought process.

For hundreds of years, the blood of innocent lambs had covered guilt. So, when John the Baptist declared, *"Behold the Lamb of God...,"* the concept of the blood was understood. But John identified that the blood of God's Lamb would accomplish what the blood of earthly lambs could never do when he declared, *"who takes away the sin of the world"* (John 1:29 NKJV).

Jesus wasn't sent to the cross as punishment for crimes He had committed. Jesus was the innocent Lamb taken by the priests and carried to the altar. The Chief Priests and temple guards were the ones who took Jesus into custody in the Garden of Gethsemane (Luke 22:52). They took Jesus to the house of the High Priest to accuse Him (Luke 22:54). The High Priest accused Jesus of blasphemy (Matthew 26:65). The High Priest then had the Chief Priest, and the elders take Jesus to Pilate for execution.

The Blood Applied to the Conscience

To be free from guilt, people needed the sacrifice of an animal's life given for them. They would watch and acknowledge that this was done *for* them. But the cleansing was an action that was done *to* them. The blood was sprinkled on them in a ceremony specifically designed for cleansing.

People identified that the blood sprinkled on them would cleanse them so that they could serve God. But, in the New Testament, a comparison is made between this cleansing by the blood of animals and the cleansing power of Jesus' blood.

The blood of goats and bulls and the ashes of cows sprinkled on unclean people made their bodies holy and clean. The blood of Christ, who had no defect, does even more. Through the eternal Spirit he offered himself to God and cleansed our consciences from the useless things we had done. Now we can serve the living God (Hebrews 9:13-14 GW).

Jesus died on the cross in our place, giving His life for us. But that is not the *only* connection we have with His blood. The blood is supposed to be the cleansing agent for our consciences. We can live free from the embarrassment of our past. We can live free from the humiliation of what we have done. We can live without the torment of what was done to us. When we learn to access this cleansing power by faith in what the Word declares, we can purge, scrub, and cleanse our thoughts, emotions, and conscience of the shame from our past.

The sprinkling of the blood is what cleanses the conscience of all shame and any feeling of yesterday's guilt. God doesn't want us to feel shame when we talk to Him. It was shame that caused Adam and Eve to draw back from God's presence and shame that caused me to draw back from God when I needed His help the most.

But Hebrews 10:22 says, *"Let us go right into the presence of God with sincere hearts fully trusting him. For our guilty consciences have been sprinkled with Christ's blood to make us clean, and our bodies have been washed with pure water"* (NLT).

When I applied the blood of Jesus to my conscience, I experienced a newfound delight in being with God. I went to pray with anticipation and joy to be with Him. Entering worship was easier than it had ever been because there was no blanket of shame. The evidence that we have applied the blood to cleanse the shame is that we have boldness to enter into the Holiest.

Having therefore, brethren, boldness to enter into the holiest by the blood of Jesus, By a new and living way, which he hath consecrated for us, through the veil, that is to say, his flesh; And having an high priest over the house of God; Let us draw near with a true heart in full assurance of faith, having our hearts sprinkled from an evil conscience, and our bodies washed with pure water (Hebrews 10:19-22).

We can boldly approach the holiest place of all—the throne of God's holy presence—because the blood has made us holy. In this passage, the word *enter* describes the entrance of a priest approaching God to serve Him. We are qualified to approach the Lord in His holy, heavenly temple, bringing sacrifices of praise and offering prayers for our families, friends, and even ourselves. The blood not only cleanses our guilt; it makes us kings and priests—able to minister to God and for God.

...Unto Him that loved us and washed us from our sins in His own blood And has made us kings and priests unto God... (Revelation 1:5-6).

The blood makes us a part of God's royal family. We can enter heaven's holiest place where Jesus, the King of the universe, is seated in His place of power. Through faith in His shed blood, we belong there. Through the blood of Jesus, we can approach our Heavenly Father and have the relationship with

Him that He has always wanted. We can come to our Heavenly Father without guilt. When our faith grasps the truth that we are free from shame, we will automatically draw near to God.

Taking Action

1. Identify the presence of any guilt or shame from your past and apply the blood of Jesus to that area of your life.

    a. Apply the blood by saying, "Father, the blood of Jesus cleanses me from all unrighteousness. I receive the shed blood of Jesus for the sin I committed. Through His blood, I am clean and justified (1 John 1:9, Romans 5:9).

    b. Walk in line with what the blood of Jesus has accomplished. In other words, act like you are clean and acceptable to your Heavenly Father. Don't come before Him groveling or reminding Him of all the things of your past. Come to Him thankful and rejoicing that you are His child.

2. *"Let us draw near..."* (Hebrews 10:22).

    a. Because we have the blood of Jesus, which provides greater access to God, we should come to Him, ask of Him, and fellowship with Him.

b. Guard that clean, intimate relationship with the Father by living holy. The blood cleanses us to set us apart to God and for God. Honor the work of the blood by keeping yourself pure from sexual sins like adultery or pornography. If you aren't married, you are not authorized to have sex. Guard what the blood has done in you.

c. Make yourself available to fulfill the plan of God. Every member of the body of Christ has a part to play in His kingdom business. The blood has made you qualified to serve the Lord.

My Declaration

I worship my Heavenly Father for everything the blood of His Lamb has supplied in my life. Through the blood of Jesus, I am redeemed from a life of sin and shame (Revelation 5:9). *Because of Jesus' blood, I am justified, pure, and holy in the presence of God* (Romans 5:9). *The blood of Jesus has made me a king and priest to God, and I can reign victoriously over the situations of my life* (Revelation 5:10). *I enter the presence of God with confidence because of the blood and I draw myself near to Him* (Hebrews 10:19,22). *As I consider the relationship I have with my Heavenly*

Father because of the blood, I rejoice. I will never be the same since Jesus Christ has washed me and cleansed me by the blood of the cross.

Praying for Someone You Love

The application of the blood of Jesus is a spiritual action of believing with the heart and declaring with the mouth (Romans 10:10). In the application of the blood of the Passover lamb in Exodus 12, the blood signaled that the people in that household were redeemed from the destruction that would come. *"Now the blood shall be a sign for you... and when I see the blood, I will pass over you; and the plague shall not be on you to destroy you..."* (Exodus 12:13 NKJV).

In the name of Jesus, I apply the blood of Jesus to the life of my loved one. I cover their mind, will, and emotions with the blood of God's Lamb. My loved one is redeemed from all destruction because the blood signals their protection. Father, I ask You to reveal to them the power Your blood provides to cleanse them from their past. Let them walk in such a clear understanding of the blood of Jesus that they approach You with confidence and joy. I pray that the blood of Jesus would purge their conscience until they see themselves as Your child, Your heir. Thank You, Lord, for what Your blood is doing to help my loved one walk in victory!

CHAPTER FIFTEEN

FUNDAMENTAL #4
PUT ON THE MIND
OF CHRIST

As I pulled out of the driveway, I went through the list in my mind. *Did I turn off the iron? Check. Did I bring my Bible? Check.* I would be on time for church if I didn't run into any slowdowns on Gallatin Road. Gliding between lanes, I made my way through the rush hour traffic with ease, thinking about the sermon series the pastor had been ministering and how it was helping my life. *I hope he continues teaching on that subject tonight,* I thought, as I put my blinker on and shifted into the turning lane.

My thoughts were abruptly diverted when the police car pulled into the turning lane behind me. My hands began to sweat profusely while my stomach twisted in knots. It felt like all the blood had rushed out of my body, and I had to remind myself to breathe. My mind raced with an onslaught of tormenting thoughts, the same thoughts I had endured for years whenever a police car pulled behind me in traffic. *What if he pulls you over? What if he runs the tags and finds they don't belong on this car? What if he asks for your insurance card? What if he searches your car and finds…?*

Suddenly, I asked myself, *What am I worried about? I am perfectly legal!* My license plates, registration, and insurance were intact. I had no drugs, alcohol, or guns in the car, just a Bible! I was sober and drug-free. If the police pulled me over, they wouldn't have any reason to arrest me and put me in jail. I was so excited! I almost wanted to get pulled over just so I could show how clean I was!

But what stopped my mind from racing and my stomach from feeling like it was tied in knots? The wrong thought caused a negative reaction of fear, while the right thought brought peace. When I replaced the previous way of thinking, I could overcome the way those thoughts were affecting me.

Out With the Old

The Bible says in 1 Corinthians 2:16, *"…we have the mind of Christ."* But what does that mean? Now that we are saved, does our mind automatically think right? Mine didn't. As a matter of fact, it maintained the same thoughts until I purposefully changed my mind. We are born again and can think like Christ *if* we exchange our thoughts for God's thoughts. I soon discovered this thought exchange was my responsibility.

The Bible says we can forsake our old ways and thoughts, accepting God's higher way of thinking in the process.

Let the wicked forsake his way, and the unrigh-teous man his thoughts: and let him return unto the Lord, and he will have mercy upon him; and to our God, for he will abundantly pardon. For my thoughts are not your thoughts, neither are your ways my ways, saith the Lord. For as the heavens are higher than the earth, so are my ways higher than your ways, and my thoughts than your thoughts (Isaiah 55:7-9).

For a few years after we moved to Kansas, I worked for a property management company. My responsibilities included painting, cleaning, and light maintenance repairs of the houses that had been vacated, preparing them for the next tenants. The previous tenants often left behind trash, broken furniture, and unwanted items. Before I could clean or do any repairs, I had to remove the trash out of the home. I went from room to room, bagging up the clothes and rubbish and removing any broken appliances or furniture. When I had succeeded in removing all of the trash left behind from the people who once lived there, it was easy to apply the fresh paint and deep clean the house to prepare for those who were moving into the home.

Before you can successfully live this new life that God has provided, you have to remove the trash that was collected by the previous tenant—the old you! This is the connection between the old life and the new.

Throw off your old sinful nature and your former way of life, which is corrupted by lust and deception. Instead, let the Spirit renew your thoughts and attitudes. Put on your new nature, created to be like God—truly righteous and holy (Ephesians 4:22-24 NLT).

The instructions in these verses are directed toward us. In verse 22, we are told to throw off the old, and in verse 24, the instruction is *"Put on the new...."* Right in the middle, we have the key: Renew the thoughts!

Let the water of God's Word wash your brain. Yes! Allow God's Word to brainwash you into thinking in line with Him. When we first began to pastor the church in Kansas, we encountered many lovely people who had been in church but not in the Word. As we taught basic principles from the Bible, one dear lady said, "I feel like I am being brainwashed but in a good way. This is God's Word. You are reading it straight from the Bible, but I've never seen it before."

One of the things she had been taught was that it was dangerous to pray for patience because God would put terrible things on you to teach you patience. We began to teach on the fruit of the Spirit from Galatians 5:22-23, and she saw that patience was placed in her heart at the new birth. She found that patience is the tool that we can pull out and put to work when difficulties arise. When we work our patience, it is developed. But patience is a supply of God to help us walk in victory and obtain the promises. That dear sister had been deprived of the help that patience provides because she thought wrong!

In Romans 12:2, we find the same instruction to renew the mind. In this verse, we can see an indication that the renewing of the mind helps us to mature spiritually.

> *And do not be conformed to this world [any longer with its superficial values and customs], but be transformed and progressively changed [as you mature spiritually] by the renewing of your mind [focusing on godly values and ethical attitudes], so that you may prove [for yourselves] what the will of God is, that which is good and acceptable and perfect [in His plan and purpose for you]* (Romans 12:2 AMP).

This text says we are *transformed and progressively changed* as we renew our minds. The transformation is like a caterpillar who becomes a butterfly. Although it began as a caterpillar, the metamorphosis provides such a change that you can't even recognize it as the same creature. The butterfly not only looks different in appearance, but it also has mobility and agility that it never knew as a caterpillar. We are designed to soar above adversity and move into God's kingdom provisions, but we must think right to live right.

Spiritually or Carnally Minded?

If the renewed mind is a spiritual mind, what do you call the mind of the Christian who has not renewed their mind? The Bible calls it a carnal mind.

> *For to be carnally minded is death; but to be spiritually minded is life and peace. Because the carnal mind is enmity against God: for it is not subject to the law of God, neither indeed can be* (Romans 8:6-7).

According to this verse, the carnal mind positions itself against the direction of God and doesn't want to follow God's plans, instructions, or leadings. I think this is what the Apostle Paul meant when he said, *"I don't really understand myself, for I want to do what is right, but I don't do it. Instead, I do what I hate"* (Romans 7:15 NLT).

I have been there! Have you? Have you ever found yourself wondering, *Why did I do that? Why did I act that way?* One day, I found myself following my husband through the house so I could get the last word. The whole time I was doing it, my heart was telling me to find a soft word that turns away wrath (Proverbs 15:1). But no! From one side of the house to the other I went, determined that he would admit I was right. Of course, I had to repent to him and to the Lord, kicking myself spiritually while asking, *Why didn't I just give a soft answer? Why did I keep the disagreement going?* I knew the answer. I was carnally minded. Thank God, I've come a long way!

Another vital purpose of renewing the mind is to shut the door to the attack of the enemy. Satan attacks through thoughts and ideas. If we have our minds renewed to God's Word, the enemy can't find an entrance or gain a stronghold.

For though we walk in the flesh, we do not war after the flesh: (For the weapons of our warfare are not carnal, but mighty through God to the pulling down of strong holds;) Casting down imaginations, and every high thing that exalteth itself against the knowledge of God, and bringing into captivity every thought to the obedience of Christ (2 Corinthians 10:3-5).

Our weapons work by pulling down, casting down, and taking thoughts captive. The list describes thoughts at various stages of development—strongholds, imaginations, thoughts that try to gain a position above God's Word, and basic thoughts.

If you bring a thought into the obedience of Christ, it will never gain the momentum to exalt itself against the knowledge of God. It won't expand into an imagination, and it will not advance to the level of a stronghold.

A stronghold consists of thought patterns that have been highly developed and entrenched in your mind. You have allowed those thoughts to process in your mind multiple times until they seem normal to you. Prejudice is a stronghold. Phobias are strongholds. An addiction is a stronghold. None of these are built by thinking that way once. While the enemy "energizes" the hate, fear, or addiction, the basis of the bondage is a thought process. The description of how our weapons work against them is "pulling down," which paints a picture of something built high in your mind.

Imaginations and thoughts that exalt themselves against the knowledge of God are at a level under a stronghold but above a basic thought. Imaginations have details like a video that plays in the mind. When my teenagers would be late coming home, I had to cast down imaginations. The mental images of all the terrible things that might have happened were running through my mind. I felt like a tennis player constantly swinging at the ball as I cast down the imaginations, time after time.

Any person who has overcome addiction can remember how the temptation started with a thought and continued into an imagination. For instance, they have been doing great all week. But when payday comes, the knowledge that money is available comes with a thought. If they don't take the thought captive, they will soon have a plan. They will think, *I can cash my check over my lunch break, drive down to the drug dealer, get high, and be back in time to finish my day.* The imagination or plan circles around in their mind, pressuring them and gaining momentum until they act on what they are imagining.

We are supposed to cast down *imaginations and every high thing that exalts itself against the knowledge of God.* What is a *high thing?* Well, what about the wind and waves that provoked thoughts in Peter, causing him to doubt the word of Jesus? So, a *high thing* can be a situation or event that tries to change our minds and convince us against the Word of God.

We should develop a spiritual alarm system that blares loudly and flashes red whenever something tries to make us move away from the Word of God. What would our lives be like today if Eve would have had an alarm system? When you read the details of how the devil attacked her, you don't see any resistance from Eve. She might as well have invited Satan to sit down and have some coffee. She made him comfortable in the conversation and allowed him to exalt his deadly lies above the loving truth of God that was once protecting her. When the imagination was playing its mental video at full force, Eve perceived things she had never considered before.

> *And when the woman saw that the tree was good for food, and that it was pleasant to the eyes, and a tree to be desired to make one wise, she took of the fruit thereof, and did eat, and gave also unto her husband with her; and he did eat* (Genesis 3:6).

Once Satan had access to Eve's thoughts, he directed her actions. When she saw or perceived it wrong, she acted in line with that wrong thought. Do you see why the Lord told us to forsake the thoughts we used to think and embrace His thoughts? God's thoughts contain God's ways, and Satan's thoughts contain Satan's ways.

So, can we bring *every* thought into obedience? Yes! The Bible says we can, so we can. And it is not as overwhelming as it sounds. If you renew the mind, you remove and replace the old, twisted thinking with sound judgment and wisdom. At that point, it is a matter of maintaining the mind, guarding it against the entrance of wrong thoughts.

A Bouncer at the Door of the Mind

I love something that Kenneth E. Hagin taught about the mind. He often remarked that renewing the mind is like combing your hair. You need to do both every day. How true! We encounter enough adverse ideas and worldly thoughts just watching the commercials on TV, much less from all the other information we deal with in our day. So, we need daily practice using the weapons of our warfare that pull down, cast down, and take thoughts captive.

> *Wherefore gird up the loins of your mind, be sober, and hope to the end for the grace that is to be brought unto you at the revelation of Jesus Christ* (1 Peter 1:13).

Notice the different way the phrase *"gird up the loins of your mind"* is translated in the following versions:

- AMPC, Brace up your minds.

- GW, Your minds must be clear and ready for action.
- WET, Put out of the way everything that would impede the free action of the mind.

The imagery produced by the words *gird* and *brace up* helps us see the restraint and restriction that we are to establish at the entrance to our thoughts. We can't allow our minds to follow certain paths or wander in the wrong direction. We don't have to accept every thought that presents itself to the mind.

The Bible gives a specific list of thoughts that are acceptable.

> *And the peace of God, which passeth all understanding, shall keep your hearts and minds through Christ Jesus. Finally, brethren, whatsoever things are true, whatsoever things are honest, whatsoever things are just, whatsoever things are pure, whatsoever things are lovely, whatsoever things are of good report; if there be any virtue, and if there be any praise, think on these things* (Philippians 4:7-8).

If the thought is not found on the list, it needs to be rejected. Like a bouncer who stands outside of a members-only club, refusing entrance to anyone who is not on the list, we need to be diligent about the thoughts we accept. When we do our part, the peace of God will keep our hearts and minds safe and secure from fear and torment.

One of my favorite verses is Isaiah 26:3 (NKJV), which says, *"You will keep him in perfect peace, whose mind is stayed on You, because he trusts in You."* The word *stayed* indicates that we place our mind upon the Lord to rest on Him. If we maintain our minds, God's supernatural restoration can continually work in our lives. I have endeavored to keep my mind stayed on God, His covenant, His promises, and His provision in Christ. I will testify that God has been faithful to restore my life and keep me in perfect peace.

Taking Action

1. Identify areas in your thought life where you have worry, dread, or fear. Prepare to take the thoughts captive before they gain momentum.

2. When the thought comes, speak the Word of God to the thought. For example, "God's Word says, 'though I walk through the valley of the shadow of death, I will fear no evil.' God is with me. No evil shall befall me, and no plague or disease will come near me" (Psalm 23:4, Psalm 91:10).

3. Be aware of thoughts that are presented through TV or social media. There are shows you shouldn't watch and people you shouldn't follow on social media. If thoughts of criticism are constantly inserted in your

mind, you will struggle walking in love. If thoughts of fear are deposited in your mind every day, you will reap a harvest of fear— even if that was not your intention.

4. Once you have pulled down the strongholds of fear, prejudice, criticism, etc., build the godly strongholds in your thought life.

   a. A stronghold of righteousness: Isaiah 54:14, 1 Corinthians 1:30, Philippians 3:9, Romans 10:3-4.

   b. A stronghold of health: Exodus 15:26, Exodus 23:25, Psalm 91:16, Psalm 103:1-4, Isaiah 53:1-5.

   c. A stronghold of peace: Isaiah 26:3, Philippians 4:7-8.

   d. A stronghold of the Blessing: Genesis 1:28, Genesis 12:1-3, Deuteronomy 28:1-14, Proverbs 10:22.

My Declaration

I submit my thoughts and perceptions to the authority of God's Word. I invite the Holy Spirit to correct me if I have any wrong thoughts that are hindering me from walking in the plan of God. I am being transformed as I renew my mind with God's Word, and I can perceive the good, acceptable, and perfect will of God in my life (Romans 12:2). *I have the mind of Christ, and I choose to keep my mind stayed on the Lord and His promises* (1 Corinthians 2:16, Isaiah 26:3). *I refuse to allow fear, worry, or discouragement to harass my mind. I reject every demonic accusation that disagrees with what the Word of God says about me. Instead, I think on the things that are true, just, pure, lovely and of good report* (Philippians 4:8). *God has given me a sound mind!*

Praying for Someone You Love

The weapons of our warfare, spoken of in 2 Corinthians 10:3-5, are available for us to use when praying for our loved ones to pull down strongholds, cast down imaginations, and take thoughts captive. We can apply spiritual pressure against the lies and deception the enemy uses against our loved ones and pray for light and clarity to be provided.

For instance, the Apostle Paul prayed in Ephesians 3:18-19 that they would be able to comprehend the dimensions of the love of Christ so they could be filled with the fullness of God. He indicated in Ephesians 4:18 that when the understanding is darkened, it causes people to be alienated from the life of God. So, let's pray for the light of God's Word to shine in the minds of our loved ones.

Father, Your Word is a lamp for our feet and a light for our paths (Psalm 119:105). *In the name of Jesus, I pray for the light produced by Your Word to shine brightly in the mind of my loved one, giving them understanding of their place in Christ and their victory over every kind of destruction* (Psalm 119:130).

In the name of Jesus, I execute authority over the mind-blinding of the enemy. I break the lies and deception of Satan from operating against them. I declare liberty to their mind to see the light. I pray that my loved one would forsake, abandon, and completely leave the unrighteous thoughts of their past and submit to Your higher thoughts (Isaiah 55:7, 9). *I pray for the peace of God that passes all understanding to mount a guard over the heart and mind of my loved one* (Philippians 4:7). *Thank You, Father, for giving my loved one a sound mind—the mind of Christ!*

CHAPTER SIXTEEN

FUNDAMENTAL #5 LEARN TO FOLLOW GOD'S SPIRIT

The way the Holy Spirit leads isn't hard to follow. He is a "professional" at leading the people of God. With His help, we can avoid every pitfall, failure, and trap. If we are following the leading of the Holy Spirit, He is leading us in provision and protection.

God's Spirit is *called* to lead us with a holy calling from our Heavenly Father, and He takes His calling seriously. Jesus used the Greek word *parakletos* to identify the role of the Holy Spirit in our lives. The second part of this compound word means "to call, summons, or appoint." It describes a holy calling like the call to be a pastor, evangelist, or prophet. The Spirit of God is appointed by God to help us in every area of our lives.

> *But the Helper, the Holy Spirit, whom the Father will send in My name, He will teach you all things, and bring to your remembrance all things that I said to you* (John 14:26 NKJV).

We need this holy help to live out God's plan. We need the things the Holy Spirit teaches, and we need His help to remember what the Lord has spoken to us. So, we should want to become skilled in learning and receiving from the Spirit of God.

The Holy Spirit is adept at doing His part if we are doing our part. But He is a gentleman. He won't force us to give Him our attention. He won't demand that we get out of bed and seek Him. Instead, the Holy Spirit is on stand-by, ready to impart, teach, lead, and enlighten us.

Following is our part. All of us can become better at following. It takes time, attention, and practice, but we can grow in this area. The Spirit of God will help us learn His voice and know how He leads.

Fullness Is God's Goal

Have you ever run out of gasoline? After a couple of times of being stranded on the side of the road, I eventually disciplined myself to look at the gas gauge. I don't drive on empty. Usually, I don't let the tank get under half a tank. We should develop the same discipline in our spiritual lives. Don't allow your spiritual supply to run low.

God instructs us to live full, and there is a good reason why! Marriage is easier if you are full of the Spirit of God. Walking in love, receiving healing, forgiving others, and receiving correction—these things are easier if you maintain fullness. Everything is easier when you are full of God.

Wherefore be ye not unwise, but understanding what the will of the Lord is. And be not drunk with wine, wherein is excess; but be filled with the Spirit (Ephesians 5:17-18).

God's design is for His children to be directed by His Spirit. Verse 18 in The New Testament: An Expanded Translation says, *"...But be constantly controlled by the Spirit."* It is much easier for the Holy Spirit to lead us when we live full.

What is the fullness of the Spirit, and how do we access that fullness? According to Scripture, the Holy Spirit lives in us and *can* come upon us. Both are in God's design for you.

If you have Him living in you, and then He comes upon you, you will reach a fullness and overflow. Like the gas tank overflows, your heart will overflow!

A Well AND Rivers

Jesus described the personal interaction we have with His Spirit as a well or a fountain: *"...But the water that I shall give him will become in him a fountain of water springing up into everlasting life"* (John 4:14 NKJV). This fountain of living water is the presence of the Holy Spirit, abiding in the spirit of every believer.

Do you not know that you are the temple of God and that the Spirit of God dwells in you? (1 Corinthians 3:16 NKJV)

> *Or do you not know that your body is the temple of the Holy Spirit who is in you, whom you have from God, and you are not your own?* (1 Corinthians 6:19 NKJV)

> *But if the Spirit of Him who raised Jesus from the dead dwells in you, He who raised Christ from the dead will also give life to your mortal bodies through His Spirit who dwells in you* (Romans 8:11 NKJV).

But He didn't stop there. Jesus also emphasized another interaction with the Holy Spirit we are supposed to have. In John 7, Jesus said we would have rivers of living water flowing through us.

> *On the last day, that great day of the feast, Jesus stood and cried out, saying, "If anyone thirsts, let him come to Me and drink He who believes in Me, as the Scripture has said, out of his heart will flow rivers of living water." But this He spoke concerning the Spirit, whom those believing in Him would receive; for the Holy Spirit was not yet given, because Jesus was not yet glorified* (John 7:37-39 NKJV).

The fountain or well is for our personal stability, but the rivers provide a supernatural flow. We need His supernatural flow! Jesus gave specific details about the power that is imparted in the rivers of living water.

Behold, I send the Promise of My Father upon you;
but tarry in the city of Jerusalem until you are endued
with power from on high (Luke 24:49 NKJV).

The word *power* is defined as "force, strength, ability, and worker of miracles." Jesus used the same word in Acts 1:8 when He said, *"But you shall receive power* (force, strength, ability, and the worker of miracles) *after that the Holy Spirit has come upon you...."*

The Lord clearly instructed us to receive this impartation of His Spirit. The disciples followed the instruction and met together, waiting for the Promise of the Father. When the Holy Spirit came upon them, they reached fullness and over-flowed. The overflow of their fullness manifested with them speaking in tongues as the Spirit gave them utterance.

When the Day of Pentecost had fully come, they
were all with one accord in one place. And suddenly
there came a sound from heaven, as of a rushing
mighty wind, and it filled the whole house where
they were sitting. Then there appeared to them
divided tongues, as of fire, and one sat upon each of
them. And they were all filled with the Holy Spirit
and began to speak with other tongues, as the Spirit
gave them utterance (Acts 2:1-4 NKJV).

We need the fullness and the utterance of the Spirit of God. Do you remember what we read from Ephesians 5:18? We are instructed to be filled. The literal Greek says, "be being filled." It refers to a continual filling by the Spirit of God and describes the spiritual utterances of psalms, hymns, and spiritual songs.

> *And be not drunk with wine, wherein is excess; but be filled with the Spirit; Speaking to yourselves in psalms and hymns and spiritual songs, singing and making melody in your heart to the Lord* (Ephesians 5:18-19).

Thankfully, I was filled with the Holy Spirit just days after I was born again. I say "thankfully" because I can look at my life and see how the fullness of the Spirit has helped me.

The spiritual songs listed in verse 19 are a great example. There are times I have been singing to the Lord, speaking in other tongues, and the answer to my problem came floating up out of my spirit.

More than once, God has used a psalm, a hymn, or a spiritual song to help me break through hindrances and redirect the course of a certain situation in my life. In Psalm 32:7, God says that He will *"compass me about with songs of deliverance."* It doesn't have to be a song in tongues. The Holy Spirit can give you a song in English too. The emphasis is that He is supernaturally supplying the utterance.

When we founded our second church campus in the Little Rock location, I needed a greater supply of strength and wisdom. We were based in De Soto, Kansas, and I drove to Little Rock every weekend.

Because I had over six hours in the car (each way), I began to use that time to pray and sing in the Spirit. Paul said in 1 Corinthians 14:16, *"...I will pray with the spirit, and I will also pray with the understanding. I will sing with the spirit, and I will also sing with the understanding"* (NKJV).

I noticed that a specific tune would come to me as I ministered to the Lord in song. The Lord told me that it was a song He had given me to bring me spiritual strength. I flowed with the utterance of the Spirit of God to the specific tune and was energized in my spirit. I continued to sing that song when I needed God's strength.

I sang that song in the Spirit for two years before the Lord gave me the interpretation of it. I was in church, about to transition from worship into the Word, when the Holy Spirit prompted me to sing my song. To my surprise, after I sang in tongues, the interpretation started bubbling up in my heart.

My Spirit Song

And though you walk down paths that have
before seemed closed before your feet
The days ahead are opening for greater and for more
More to come in glory and more to come in light
What I have in store is more to come
Chorus
And more to come, and more to
come, and more to come
And greater still, and greater still, and greater still

Verse 2

Every path I have designed that I
have laid before your feet
Every path is full of blessing and My very best
Walk ahead and walk with confidence into My plan
Because in Me you have more than victory

Verse 3

The strength to walk on higher ground
flows freely from My throne
Higher plans and higher paths are available in Me
Boldly enter into what I have chosen for your life
Walk in glory and in victory

Following the Leading

I cannot overemphasize how much we need the help of the Holy Spirit. There are specific times in my life that I can point to and say, "The leading of the Holy Spirit rescued me." I want to show you some examples of His supernatural leading from the Bible before I share some of the ways He has rescued me.

One of my favorite examples is when the Lord directed Paul and Silas on their missionary journey. In this example, we can see how the Holy Spirit will work with us.

> *Then they passed through Phrygia and the Galatian region, having been forbidden by the Holy Spirit to speak the Word in Asia. And having come down to the borders of Mysia, by a trial-and-error*

method they kept on attempting to discover whether it was right to go to Bithynia. But the Spirit of Jesus did not permit them to do so. And having skirted Mysia they came down to Troas. And a vision appeared to Paul during the night. A certain man, a Macedonian, was standing and begging him and saying, Come over into Macedonia at once and give us aid. And when he had seen the vision, immediately we endeavored to go forth into Macedonia, concluding that God had called us to tell them the good news (Acts 16:6-10 WET).

Did you notice the phrase "trial-and-error method"? Paul and Silas were "attempting to discover" the direction the Lord wanted them to go. They knew when they hit a "red light" and stopped. But they had to continue checking with the Holy Spirit to see if their next direction was the right direction. Finally, the Holy Spirit used a vision to convey the specific detail Paul and Silas needed.

The Holy Spirit wants us to move forward in what we know to be the will of God. That is why we start with the Word as our foundation. We learn to recognize the voice of God as He speaks to us through His Word.

But when it comes to specific details that aren't covered by Scripture, we are not left to figure it out on our own. No! We have the Holy Spirit in His fullness—in us and on us! His supernatural manifestations will rescue us!

A Pivotal Decision

I found out the hard way how difficult things can be when I am not maintaining a spiritual fullness. It was a pivotal time in our ministry, and if I had not followed the Lord to make some corrections, I would have lost the ministry God had planned for me.

It seemed like the enemy attacked from every side. One of our kids was making wrong choices and causing chaos in our home. At the same time, three young families in the church decided to backslide and began to drink at a local karaoke bar. This caused the other people in the church to wonder what happened to them. The church finances were struggling because of the shift in income, and we were struggling to adjust the church budget.

At the time, I was low on spiritual strength. I wasn't feeding on the Word like I should have been. I wasn't casting down imaginations or taking thoughts captive. On the contrary, I allowed thoughts of worry to run rampant in my mind. Instead of being filled with all joy and peace in believing (Romans 15:13), I was full of doubt and fear in despairing.

I decided to give up my paycheck and go to work at night. My choice was born out of reasoning and the pressure of the situation. The Holy Spirit was not involved in my decision. I was living my Christian life in the flesh, dealing with the difficulties by using carnal instruments.

During the forty-five-minute trip to my evening shift, I had worship playing, I was singing, and my tears were flowing. It may have appeared that I was doing something spiritual, but my "worship" was motivated by my flesh. It was emotional instead of spiritual, moving me deeper into sadness. I was telling the Lord how horrible things were in my life, begging Him to help me when suddenly the Holy Spirit spoke to me.

He said, "If you don't work the Word the way you have been taught, you are going to forfeit everything I have planned for you."

At that moment, I saw a vision of dominoes neatly stacked in a line. As the first domino fell, the entire line followed, one by one until it came to the last domino. Then, the Holy Spirit explained, "If you let go of faith in this situation, it will have a domino effect, causing you to eventually question your salvation."

The words the Holy Spirit spoke to me that evening shook me out of the stupor of self-pity and doubt. I dried my eyes and took a sober look at my spiritual condition. I wasn't operating in faith. I had reacted to the situation out of my mind and emotions without consulting the Word of God or the help of the Holy Spirit.

I picked up the Word and began to build my faith. Within the month, I was back working at the church, taking a paycheck when the money was there and sowing my time to the Lord when it wasn't. That month, a proposal was offered for me to host my own television program. As I sat at my desk, looking at the offer, my husband walked into my office and asked, "Do you think you should sign the contract?"

Without consulting my head, I answered from my spirit, "I don't have the option not to sign it." I picked up the ink pen and signed the contract, committing to pay for a year's worth of airtime and the production. We began our broadcast, *Faith Builders with Philip and Michelle Steele*, in 2010 and have been ministering through television since that time, expanding to include a Spanish broadcast.

I praise the Lord for His mercy, but I have learned from that mistake. I learned that life is easier if I live full of God. I endeavor to maintain a continual fullness of the Spirit of God. I check my joy levels often and charge my joy by being thankful and rejoicing. I guard my peace by casting all of my cares on the Lord. I feed on the Word of God and put myself in His presence as a student who has much to learn.

Promptings and Perceptions

We shouldn't demand a spectacular leading from the Holy Spirit. Many times, the Spirit of God will softly prompt us. Romans 8:16 describes the leading by saying, *"The Spirit Himself bears witness with our spirit that we are children of God."*

When Luke wrote his Gospel account, he said, *"It seemed good to me...to write unto thee...."* Peter made the statement in explaining Scripture, *"...but holy men of God spake as they were moved by the Holy Ghost"* (2 Peter 1:21). The leading of the Holy Spirit is not always dramatic. Sometimes it is a prompting or a perception.

Paul was being led by the Spirit to warn the captain of the ship not to sail into the storm. He said, *"Sirs, I perceive that this voyage will be with hurt and much damage, not only of the lading and ship, but also of our lives"* (Acts 27:10). Paul was picking that up in his spirit like a pilot can read a radar screen and see an impending storm.

On one of the occasions when I was driving from Little Rock to Kansas, I felt prompted to stop and fuel up. I looked down at my fuel gauge, but it was three-quarters full. I had just fueled at my last stop. The prompting came to me again with a simple idea, "It doesn't hurt to top it off." I followed the prompting, knowing it was from the Lord. It only took a few minutes to fill the tank. I got back into my car and continued toward Kansas City. As I approached Harrisonville, I knew why the Lord prompted me. The accident littered the road. It was so recent the first responders had not yet arrived. If I had not stopped, it could have been me. Thank You, Lord, for the rescue of the Holy Spirit.

One day, my husband marched up the stairs like a man on a mission. From the look on his face, I knew he was concerned. Immediately, I asked, "What is wrong?"

He told me that the Lord had directed him to look in one of the drawers in our teenager's room. The Lord specifically said, "Look in the top drawer, in the back, righthand corner."

I followed him into the room. He pulled out the drawer, and there in the right-hand corner was a pack of cigarettes and lighter! Busted!

I experienced a similar leading with another one of our teenagers. Before church, she said she wasn't feeling well, so I allowed her to stay home. I was leading praise and worship, and my husband was preaching that day. As soon as I finished worship and handed the service to him, the Holy Spirit said, "Get your keys and go home NOW!"

I told my assistant, "I have to go to my house right now." She climbed in the car, and we drove to my house. As I pulled onto my street, I saw a car in my driveway that I didn't recognize. I walked in the house in time to catch an adult who was planning something inappropriate with my teenager. I came home just in time!

Those are dramatic, lifesaving examples. But the Holy Spirit helps me every day. The decisions we make about our ministry are filled with times that He directs us to do something specific. I can play "connect the dots" by looking back to see that this decision led us to this door of favor, which directed us to this relationship, etc.

The bottom line is this: you need everything the Holy Spirit is called to bring into your life. You need His fullness and supernatural help. Make it your aim to be His best student!

Take Action

1. Recognize the position the Holy Spirit is appointed to have in your life by feeding on

the following Scriptures. The Holy Spirit is here to:

a. Teach us all things (John 14:26).

b. Bring the Word of God to our remembrance (John 14:26).

c. Reprove the world (John 16:8).

d. Guide us into truth (John 16:13).

e. Speak what He hears from God (John 16:13).

f. Show us things to come (John 16:13).

g. Glorify Jesus (John 16:14).

2. If you are saved, the Holy Spirit lives in your heart. But Jesus said the Spirit of God would also come on you to give you power and bring His supernatural gifts into your life. Meditate on the following verses and open your heart to receive His fullness.

    a. Jesus is the One who baptizes in the Holy Ghost and fire (Matthew 3:11, Mark 1:8, Luke 3:16, John 1:32-34).

    b. The Holy Spirit came UPON Jesus (John 1:32-34).

    c. Jesus identified the "Promise of the Father" as the baptism of the Holy Spirit (Luke 24:49, Acts 1:2-5).

d. When the people were filled, they spoke with other tongues (Acts 2:1-4, Acts 10:44-46).

My Declaration

The Spirit of God dwells in me and leads me (Romans 8:11, 14). Because the Comforter, the Holy Spirit, is living in my heart, I can hear directly from God. I am never without God's presence to guide me and instruct in the decisions I need to make. The Holy Spirit is my Teacher. I submit to His leadership, committing to respond in faith immediately when the Spirit of God prompts me to do something (John 14:26). The Holy Spirit guides me into all truth and shows me things to come (John 16:13). As I follow Him, I will be safe from deception and aware of God's plans for me.

I receive the fullness of the Holy Spirit and His power (Acts 1:8). As I am constantly being filled with the Holy Spirit, I speak in tongues and glorify God (Ephesians 5:18, Acts 2:11). I cooperate with the gifts of the Holy Spirit as He wills and am a witness of Jesus Christ.

God has prepared things for me that my eyes haven't seen, and my ears haven't heard. The Holy Spirit is revealing these things to me (1 Corinthians 2:9-10).

*He is showing me everything that belongs to Jesus
because I am an heir of God and a joint heir with
Jesus Christ* (John 16:15, Romans 8:17).

Praying for Someone You Love

*Father, the help Your Holy Spirit provides is so
needful to help my loved one receive from You and
walk in Your plan. In the name of Jesus, I pray
for them to recognize the leading and guiding of
Your Spirit. As they accept Jesus as Lord, they are
born of Your Spirit* (John 3:8), *and according to
Romans 8:16, Your Holy Spirit will bear witness with my loved one that they are Your child
and You have given them an inheritance. I ask
in agreement with Ephesians 1:17-19 that You
would give them the spirit of wisdom and revelation in the knowledge of Jesus Christ. According to
Ephesians 3:16, I ask You to strengthen my loved
one by Your Spirit in their inner man. I thank
You, Father, that the Spirit of Truth will guide
them into all truth and will glorify Jesus to my
loved one.*

PRAYER OF SALVATION

Dear Heavenly Father:

I come to You in the Name of Jesus. Your Word says, "...that if you confess with your mouth the Lord Jesus and believe in your heart that God has raised Him from the dead, you will be saved. You also said, "whoever calls on the name of the LORD shall be saved" (Romans 10:9, 13 NKJV).

I believe in my heart that Jesus Christ is the Son of God. I believe Jesus died for my sins and was raised from the dead. I am calling upon His Name, the Name of Jesus. Father, I know that You saved me now.

Your Word says, "...For with the heart one believes unto righteousness, and with the mouth confession is made unto salvation" (Romans 10:10 NKJV).

I do believe with my heart, and I confess Jesus now as my Lord. Therefore, I am saved! Thank You, Father.

How To Be Filled with the Holy Spirit

A cts 2:38 (NKJV) says, *"...Repent, and let every one of you be baptized in the name of Jesus Christ for the remission of sins; and you shall receive the gift of the Holy Spirit."* The Holy Spirit is given to us, the children of God, by our Heavenly Father.

Jesus told His disciples, *"But you shall receive power when the Holy Spirit has come upon you; and you shall be witnesses to Me..."* (Acts 1:8 NKJV). When we are baptized with the Holy Spirit, we receive supernatural power that enables us to live victoriously.

The Holy Spirit IN and ON the Believer

When we are born again, we receive the indwelling of the Person of the Holy Spirit. Romans 8:16 (NKJV) tells us, *"The Spirit Himself bears witness with our spirit that we are children of God."* When we are born again, we know it because the Spirit bears witness with our own spirit that we are a child of God; He confirms it to us. He is able to bear witness with your spirit because He lives inside of you; you are *indwelt* by the Spirit of God.

But Jesus speaks of another experience that follows the new birth in Acts 1:8, "...*when the Holy Spirit has come upon you.*" This interaction with the Spirit of God belongs to every believer.

God wants you to be full and overflowing with His Spirit. Being filled with the Spirit is like being full of water. Just because you had one drink of water doesn't mean you're full of water. At the new birth, you received the indwelling of the Spirit—a drink of water. But now God wants you to be filled to overflowing—be filled or baptized with the Holy Spirit.

> *And when the day of Pentecost was fully come, they were all with one accord in one place. And suddenly there came a sound from heaven as of a rushing mighty wind, and it filled all the house where they were sitting. And there appeared unto them cloven tongues like as of fire, and it sat upon each of them And they were all filled with the Holy Ghost, and began to speak with other tongues, as the Spirit gave them utterance* (Acts 2:1-4).

When the disciples were filled with the Holy Spirit, they began to speak with other tongues. The Holy Spirit gave them utterance, and they spoke in a language unknown to them. Today, when a believer is filled with the Holy Ghost, they will speak with other tongues too. These are not words that come from the mind of man, but they are words given by the Holy Spirit.

What is the benefit of being filled with the Holy Spirit with the evidence of speaking in other tongues? First Corinthians 14:2 (NKJV) reads, *"For he who speaks in a tongue does not speak to men but to God...."* Speaking in other tongues is a divine way of communicating with your Heavenly Father. This is one of many great benefits.

Once you receive the gift of the Holy Spirit, you can yield to this gift any time, speaking in other tongues as often as you choose; you don't have to wait for God to move on you. The more you speak in other tongues, the more you will benefit from this gift. By continuing to speak in other tongues on a daily basis, you will be able to maintain a Spirit-filled life; you will live full of the Spirit.

PRAYER TO RECEIVE THE HOLY SPIRIT

Father, I see that the gift of the Holy Spirit belongs to me because I am Your child. I come to You to receive this gift. I receive the gift of the Holy Spirit by faith in the same way that I received Jesus as my Lord by faith. I believe I receive the Holy Spirit now! I believe I will speak in other tongues as the Spirit gives me utterance, just like those in Acts 2 on the Day of Pentecost. Thank You for filling me with the Holy Spirit.

As the words the Spirit of God gives you float up from your heart, you must open your mouth and speak those words out. The words will not come to your mind, but they will float up from your spirit. Speak those words out.

ABOUT MICHELLE STEELE

Pastor Michelle Steele knows God's life-changing power from firsthand experience. Her zeal to spread the Word stems from how Jesus miraculously delivered her from a life of destruction and addiction. Today, Michelle, and her husband, Pastor Philip Steele, co-pastor churches in De Soto, Kansas, and Little Rock, Arkansas. In addition, Michelle hosts *Faith Builders,* a television program provided in English and Spanish that airs on Victory Television Network and Almavision Christian Network. The Steeles make their home in Little Rock and are the parents of five children.

![Harrison House logo]

Equipping Believers to Walk in the Abundant Life
John 10:10b

Connect with us on

 Facebook @ HarrisonHousePublishers

and Instagram @ HarrisonHousePublishing

so you can stay up to date with news

about our books and our authors.

Visit us at **www.harrisonhouse.com**